What is *Feng Shui* ?

Dr Evelyn Lip

What is *Feng Shui*?

ACADEMY EDITIONS

Dedicated to my son, Kenny, and my daughter, Jacqueline.

Acknowledgements

Since I started writing about the art of feng shui *in 1978, I have received positive feedback and tremendous support from my readers. To them, a big 'thank you'.*

During the course of writing this book several friends gave me much encouragement and moral support. I wish to acknowledge a few, namely Dr KW Loke, Wong Swee Hoon, ET Sinclair, Lilac Tan and PG Chua. I also wish to acknowledge Professor Foo for his encouragement.

I am appreciative and thankful to Maggie Toy for having invited me to write this architectural feng shui *book as one of the* What is . . . *series which have been most successfully published by the Academy Group. I am indebted to Lucy Ryan and Ramona Khambatta for having read the final draft of this book and for having made excellent suggestions to make the book more readable, and to Andrea Bettella, Mario Bettella and Marie Carter for finalising the design. I am grateful to them all for their invaluable advice.*

Last, but by no means least, a special word of appreciation to my immediate family, Francis, Kenny and Jacqueline, for their unceasing moral support during the course of writing this book.

COVER: Foster and Partners, Exterior view of the Hongkong and Shanghai Banking Corporation, Hong Kong (photo: Ian Lambot)

PAGE 2: Interior of the Qinian Dian (Hall of Prayers for a Good Year), Tiantan, Beijing, China. Powerful *feng shui* and symbolism are expressed in the roof structure and decoration: circular roofs refer to the heavens and infinity; cloud motifs symbolise imperial power over the universe; and the *yang* images of dancing golden dragons and the phoenix appear in sculptures and paintings on caissons and gold panels.

First published in Great Britain in 1997 by
ACADEMY EDITIONS
An imprint of

ACADEMY GROUP LTD
42 Leinster Gardens, London W2 3AN
Member of the VCH Publishing Group

ISBN: 1 85490 491 4

Distributed to the trade in the USA by
NATIONAL BOOK NETWORK, INC
4720 Boston Way, Lanham, Maryland 20706

Printed and bound in Singapore

CONTENTS

PREFACE

What is *feng shui*? What is its relevance to buildings? How does one practise *feng shui*? What is the architecture of *feng shui* buildings? This study aims to answer the above and many other questions on *feng shui*. By adopting a practical, tangible approach, the mystery of an ancient art-form – safeguarded by Orientals for centuries – will be unravelled, understanding of *feng shui* theory and practice will be heightened and the reader will be left with a clear view of the discipline from an architectural perspective.

Feng shui is the art of placement, a skill used to address the built and natural environments; a knowledge that contributes greatly when dealing with the natural forces on earth. It is a complex subject involving many disciplines, ranging from site planning to psychology. A perfect *feng shui* model is said to be blessed with *tianning, dili renhe* (the heavens send blessings, earth prosperity and people in harmony). Every individual, work place and nation needs to have auspicious *feng shui* for peace of mind, success and prosperity.

The Chinese have always believed that one's success is determined by five areas of influences: *yiming* (destiny); *eryun* (the lucky and unlucky eras); *san feng shui* (the art of placement or *feng shui*); *shi daode* (virtue) and *wu dushu* (everything that concerns oneself, such as inheritance and family background, as well as everything one undertakes, such as education, experience, exposure etc). The first two areas are not within the control of any individual or company; thus, it is of vital importance to ensure that the third, fourth and fifth areas are not overlooked but rather developed to their maximum potential. With today's stressful working environment and highly competitive society, every ambitious person requires good *feng shui* for his living and work place. In the increasingly complex and competitive arena of international and local business, auspicious *feng shui* in the marketplace is needed more than ever before.

Everyone and every business establishment is housed in a building whose form and space, structure and finish, orientation and siting react with the forces of nature and is influenced by its environment. Educated clients of

figure 1 – The Zhong Hedian of the Gugong

architects and builders have their own value system and ways of evaluating form, space and structure. In spite of technological advances, many Oriental clients still regard *feng shui* as one of the most important aspects of design and planning. Thus, the architecture of a building must have close links with the positive workings of *feng shui*. The tangible aspects such as space and form, lighting and ventilation, planning and circulation must be complemented by the intangible aspects (*feng shui*) of architecture. The *qi* (energy) and magnetism of the earth, the symbolism of shapes with reference to the Five Elements, and the nature of the site must be in harmony with nature for the users to reap the benefits of auspicious *feng shui*.

The greenhouse effect, deforestation and increasing global pollution must encourage man to adopt a more proactive attitude towards the preservation of the natural as well as built environment. *Feng shui*, practised in the correct manner, certainly helps man to focus on achieving harmony and balance in nature, to respect site constraints and live harmoniously with natural forces. No wonder *feng shui* has evolved from a mere Oriental art of siting into an international medium and environmental tool for design on micro and macro scales. Renowned schools of architecture in major universities, such as Harvard, have produced PhD or Masters graduates who have carried out in-depth studies of *feng shui*. Learned scholars such as Joseph Needham and WT De Bary have written about this aspect of Chinese culture, and the highly respected architect Sir Norman Foster designs with reference to *feng shui* precepts – for example, two escalators were moved so that they did not confront the main door of his Hongkong and Shanghai Bank.

This book is written for men and women from all walks of life, for designers and technocrats, architects and engineers, small companies and large corporations. It is broadly divided into four parts and is illustrated

figure 2 – Attributes in Chinese astrology

with many of my own sketches, which help to integrate the tangible and intangible aspects of architecture. The first section presents an introduction to the subject of *feng shui*, an overview of available source materials and literature, and the definition of *feng shui* terms. The relationship of the *Luoshu* and the Trigrams, and how these instruments are used for the assessment of *feng shui*, is also discussed.

The landscape around buildings, the shape and plan of the constructions, and the colour schemes used in interior design are briefly introduced in part two of the book. Most interestingly, perhaps, is how the *feng shui* of a building can be assessed and how the *Bazhai Mingjin* and the *Feixing* methods are applied. This exploration is complemented by numerous case studies of residential, commercial and public buildings from around the world.

Part three of this book focuses on one methodology of *feng shui* practice, through which readers may attempt to assess the *feng shui* of their own homes. Admittedly, the practice of *feng shui* is like the practice of all other forms of art and architecture; maturity, exposure and experience in the art are prerequisites to successful practice and project implementation. This section of the book also presents the *feng shui* analysis of many interesting classical Eastern and Western buildings. The *feng shui* of the burial ground for imperial Ming and Qing rulers is also described to highlight the rule of thumb for auspicious burial sites.

Part four contains information on the architectural treatment of a *feng shui* building, such as overall design concepts, details for structural and interior design and the appropriate use of lighting, finishes and furniture. A brief discussion of the influence of electrical appliances and noise created by machinery or man is followed by a short introduction to *feng shui* colours and use of appropriate colour schemes. Finally, consideration is given to the significance of symbolic elements and art work in buildings.

Year	Animal	Element
10/02/1948 - 28/01/1949	Rat	fire
28/01/1960 - 14/02/1961		earth
15/02/1972 - 02/02/1973		wood
02/02/1984 - 19/02/1985		gold
19/02/1996 - 06/02/1997		water
29/01/1949 - 16/02/1950	Ox	fire
15/02/1961 - 04/02/1962		earth
03/02/1973 - 23/01/1974		wood
20/02/1985 - 08/02/1986		gold
07/02/1997 - 27/01/1998		water
17/02/1950 - 05/02/1951	Tiger	wood
05/02/1962 - 24/01/1963		gold
24/01/1974 - 10/02/1975		water
09/02/1986 - 28/01/1987		fire
28/01/1998 - 15/02/1999		earth
06/02/1951 - 26/01/1952	Rabbit	wood
25/01/1963 - 12/02/1964		gold
11/02/1975 - 30/01/1976		water
29/01/1987 - 16/02/1988		fire
16/02/1999 - 04/02/2000		earth
08/02/1940 - 26/01/1941	Dragon	gold
27/01/1952 - 13/02/1953		water
13/02/1964 - 01/02/1965		fire
31/01/1976 - 17/02/1977		earth
17/02/1988 - 05/02/1989		wood
27/01/1941 - 14/02/1942	Snake	gold
14/02/1953 - 02/02/1954		water
02/02/1965 - 20/02/1966		fire
18/02/1977 - 06/02/1978		earth
06/02/1989 - 26/01/1990		wood
15/02/1942 - 14/02/1943	Horse	wood
03/02/1954 - 23/01/1955		gold
21/02/1966 - 08/02/1967		water
07/02/1978 - 27/01/1979		fire
27/01/1990 - 14/02/1991		earth
05/02/1943 - 24/01/1944	Goat	wood
24/01/1955 - 11/02/1956		gold
09/02/1967 - 29/01/1968		water
28/01/1979 - 15/02/1980		fire
15/02/1991 - 03/02/1992		earth
25/01/1944 - 12/02/1945	Monkey	water
12/02/1956 - 30/01/1957		fire
30/01/1968 - 16/02/1969		earth
16/02/1980 - 04/02/1981		wood
04/02/1992 - 22/01/1993		gold
13/02/1945 - 01/02/1946	Rooster	water
31/01/1957 - 17/02/1958		fire
17/02/1969 - 05/02/1970		earth
05/02/1981 - 24/01/1982		wood
23/01/1993 - 09/02/1994		gold
02/02/1946 - 21/01/1947	Dog	earth
18/02/1958 - 07/02/1959		wood
06/02/1970 - 26/01/1971		gold
25/01/1982 - 12/02/1983		water
10/02/1994 - 30/01/1995		fire
22/01/1947 - 09/02/1948	Pig	earth
08/02/1959 - 27/01/1960		wood
27/01/1971 - 14/02/1972		gold
13/02/1983 - 01/02/1984		water
31/01/1995 - 18/02/1996		fire

PART ONE

WHAT IS *FENG SHUI*?

INTRODUCTION

Feng shui is the art of placing a habitat, a house, a commercial complex, a factory or a multi-storey office block on a site so that it is in harmony with other man-made structures and in balance with nature. It is a discipline deeply rooted in Chinese cosmology and embedded in Oriental culture. The Ancient Chinese believed that the universe was made from the union of *yin* and *yang* elements and, indeed, that everything under the sky could be classified under these two elements. The earth, the moon, darkness, night, the female and the valley are *yin*, while the heavens, the sun, light, day, the male and the hill are *yang*. *Wanwu* (everything under the sky) is symbolised by the signs of the *Taiji* and the Eight Trigrams *(fig **4**)*.

It is evident that creatures in nature seek shelters that best protect them and provide them with a sense of wellbeing and security. Birds migrate to warmer climes and man seeks shelter in a place that offers protection from the wind and rain. If he lives in a damp and unventilated space, he is likely to suffer from rheumatism and other illnesses in later life. If he lives in a cold region of the northern hemisphere with northerly winds, he is best protected from the elements by a habitat sited on raised ground with a hill to the north, behind his habitat. Clearly, man's living environment is of great importance to his happiness and wellbeing.

Feng shui is indeed the art of siting, the skill of design with reference to the physical land form, climatic conditions, geographical location, and so on. For example, in Beijing where the cold, dusty winds come from the north, it is advantageous to have the windows and doors of buildings facing south with solid north-facing walls to avoid the dust and cold. A building would be equally protected from the cold wind if sheltered behind by a hill. *Feng shui* is best applied to the interior as well as the exterior design of a building so that harmony and balance are achieved and the surrounding environment is addressed appropriately and with sensitivity.

For centuries, Chinese scholars have investigated and written about the theory of *feng shui*. By the last quarter of the twentieth century, Western

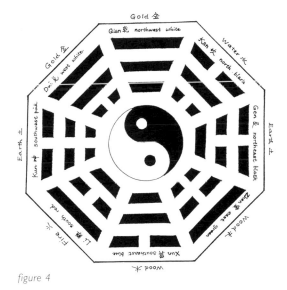

figure 4

figure 3 – Tower blocks of Fire and Earth Elements

scholars and people from all backgrounds have not only become aware of this Oriental practice, but also immensely interested in its theory and application. Dr Joseph Needham, the author of *Science and Civilization in China*, said that *feng shui* was the result of the moulding influences of wind and water. Other Western scholars define it as the rudiments of Chinese natural science. In my previous studies of *feng shui*, Chinese architecture and culture, it has been established that *feng shui* is the art of placement of buildings and matter on the earth so that they are in harmony with the natural forces such as the wind and rain.

Feng shui was first practised in China thousands of years ago. Since then, it has been firmly incorporated into traditional Chinese architecture and culture. The design principles of traditional buildings were based on concepts of *feng shui*, such as symmetry, balance, hierarchy of height, wall enclosures and auspicious orientation. As early as the third century, a Chinese dictionary had records of choosing such sites for building purposes. Literature dating back to the Zhou dynasty, containing records of choosing sites for new cities, were the *Shujing* (the Book of Documents) and the *Shijing* (the Book of Songs). Emperors from the Five Dynasties to the Qing dynasty were buried in tombs on hilly sites facing the south, for example, in Luozhou Xian. Dayu, the emperor of the Xia dynasty, chose to be buried in the auspicious site in Huiji. Qinshi Huangdi, who began preparations for his mausoleum soon after ascending the throne, chose the hilly northern part of Lishan as his final resting place. The Ming and Qing tombs can still be visited today.

Undoubtedly, the art of *feng shui* includes understanding the many facets of Chinese beliefs and culture, such as the application of the theory of *yin* and *yang*, Chinese philosophy, the significance of Chinese symbolism and the theory of magnetism. Although *feng shui* has stood the test of time and has been practised by the forefathers of the Chinese for almost three thousand years as an ancient art, its theory and practice are not as well documented as other forms of art. The rudiments of *feng shui* and the methodology of practice are closely guarded by those who are truly knowledgeable, and misunderstood by those who have only a superficial understanding. In ancient times *feng shui* was regarded as a form of biogeography. During the Qing dynasty, *feng shui* practitioners were called *dilijia* or geographers. The assessment of a *feng shui* situation was made with reference to the cosmological, environmental and earthly happenings. The classical name for *feng shui* was *kanyu*, which meant *tiandao* (the ways of the heavens) and *didao* (the ways of the earth). The first compass invented was called *piao* (floating or rotating) because it consisted of a magnetic spoon which rotated but always settled due north. From this simple magnetic compass, dating to the time of the Han dynasty, the complicated geomancer's compass was invented which comprised several rings which included the directions represented by the Eight Trigrams, the Ten Heavenly Stems, the Five Elements and the Twelve Earthly Branches. Over time it developed into a complicated thirty-six-tiered compass which gave indications of space and time in geomantic assessments.

LITERATURE ON *FENG SHUI*

One of the earliest works on *feng shui*, *Zhuanjing* (the Book of Burial), was written by an East Jin scholar, Guopu (317-420), and described the *feng shui* of burial places. Ancient literature such as *Shangshu* and *Zhouli* (classics of the Zhou dynasty from 11-3BC) also contained information on this art form. During the period of the Han dynasty (206BC to AD220), Bangu, author of *Hanshu* (records of the Han dynasty) and *Yiwen Zhi* (essays on art and literature) wrote and discussed the workings of the Five Elements and the harmony of *yin* and *yang*; while the scholars Dongzhong Shu, Liuxiang and Weinan Zi wrote about the productivity and the destructibility of the Five Elements. Several books such as *Songshi Yiwen Zhi* (records of literature of song) and *Xiangzhai Jing* (a *feng shui* classic) were published during the Song dynasty (960-1279). These books elaborated on the workings of the Elements and the *yin/yang* theory. Other well known ancient literature includes *Huangdi Erzhai Jing* (on imperial residences), *Didian Zhaijing* (on the siting of building), *Sanyuan Zhaijing* (another *feng shui* classic), *Kongzi Zhaijing* (a Confucian classic on house design), *Zhaijing* (on house design), *Weinan Zizhai Jing* (a classic on house design by Wei), *Bagua Zhaijing* (on the house and Trigrams) *Liushi Sigua Zhaijing* (on the house and Hexagrams), *Lucai Zhaijing* (on house design by Lu) and *Wuxiao Zhaijing* (on the five rules of house design). *Zhaijing* illustrated the meaning of the twenty-four orientations in *feng shui* divinations. During the South Song era, Zhuxi, a philosopher and educationalist (1130-1200), spoke of *feng shui* as the art of landscaping; the formation of land, flow of rivers and topographical features comprised the *feng shui* of a place. The 675th volume of *Gujin Tushu Jicheng* (records from ancient to present times), compiled during the Qing dynasty, also contained substantial information on *feng shui* theory.

A popular book, *Bazhai Mingjing* (the enlightening mirror of the eight houses), presents a system of *feng shui* based on the assessment of the birth date of the owner of a building. From this, the *Minggua* (the horoscope of life) of the owner can be obtained, and based on this, the orientation of the building is determined.

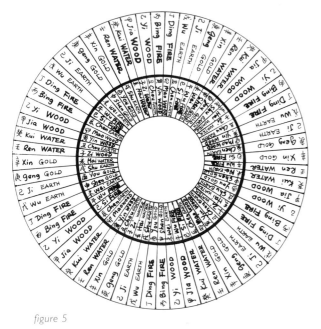

figure 5

Literature in English on *feng shui*, however, does not date back to ancient times. Joseph Needham specifically mentioned the art of *feng shui* in his publication of 1954, *Science and Civilization in China*. He recognised the fact that *feng shui* concerned the intangible aspects of Chinese architecture. My book *Chinese Geomancy* (1979) was the earliest book written in English on the practice of *feng shui* and the design and orientation of buildings. Following this, several books were published on the *feng shui* of homes and other buildings.

The concept that man benefits from the balance of *yin* and *yang* in all things is based on cosmological theory, while the concept of the harmony in the workings of the Five Elements is seen in the physical world and in nature. According to the Chinese sages, everything in the physical world can be classified under the Five Elements of *Jin* (Gold), *Mu* (Wood), *Shui* (Water), *Huo* (Fire) and *Tu* (Earth). These elements are closely associated with matter and forces in nature. Gold is represented by the west, autumn, and the colour white; Wood by the east, spring and the colour green; Water by the north, winter and the colour black; Fire by the south, summer and the colour red; and Earth by the central position and the colour yellow. Just like the seasonal changes, the Five Elements work in cyclical motions and succeed one another in a cycle of either compatible or incompatible interaction. Compatible elements are: Gold with Water; Water with Wood; Wood with Fire; Fire with Earth; Earth with Gold. Incompatible Elements are: Earth with Water; Water with Fire; Fire with Gold; Gold with Wood; Wood with Earth.

The Chinese calendar is based on the *Ganzi* (Stems and Branches) system in which the *Gan* (the Ten Heavenly Stems) are combined with the *Zi* (Twelve Earthly Branches) to form the cyclical sixty lunar recurrent years *(fig 5)*. The *Ganzi* system is devised so that each year is associated with an astrological animal symbol. This system was started by the minister of the first emperor of China in 2697BC.

North Song dynasty politician and philosopher Wang Anshi presented a comprehensive picture of how various matter in nature and the affairs of man are associated with the Five Elements:

WOOD	FIRE	EARTH	GOLD	WATER
east	south	centre	west	north
spring summer	late summer	autumn	winter	
wind	heat	moisture	drought	cold
green	red	yellow	white	black
sour	bitter/sweet	bitter/sweet	salty	
straight	sharp square	round	crooked	
azure dragon	red bird	yellow dragon	white tiger	tortoise
goat	rooster	ox	dog	pig
eye	tongue/mouth	nose	ear	
anger	happiness	thinking	sadness	fear
muscle	pulse	flesh	skin/hair	bone

figure 6

Each of the *Jiazi Nian* (the first year of the sixty-year cycle) consists of a Heavenly Stem and an Earthly Branch. For example, the year *Jiazi* is made up of *Jia* – a unit of the Heavenly Stem – and *Zi* – a unit of the Earthly Branch. The Stem *Jia* is of Wood Element while *Zi* is of Water Element.

THE EIGHT TRIGRAMS AND YIN/YANG

The numerals of the Eight Trigrams were ancient symbols attributed to China's first legendary emperor, Fuxi (2852BC). The numerals are made up of *yin*, a broken sign (- -) and *yang*, a continuous sign (—). Each Trigram is made up of three numerals of either *yin* or *yang* or a mixture of *yin* and *yang*. The Trigrams are *Qian, Kun, Zhen, Kan, Gen, Xun, Li* and *Dui. Qian* is represented by three solid lines and signifies the heavens, masculinity and the direction northwest; *Kun*, shown as three broken lines, represents the earth, femininity and the direction southwest; *Zhen*, represented by two broken lines and a solid line, indicates change and the east direction; *Kan*, represented by a solid line sandwiched by two broken lines, indicates danger and refers to the north; *Gen*, represented by a solid and two broken lines, refers to mountains and the northeast; *Xun*, shown as two solid lines and one broken one, indicates the southeast and the wind; *Li*, denoted by a broken line between two solid lines, indicates the south and is associated with the sun, lightning and fire, and *Dui*, indicated by one broken and two solid lines, denotes west and signifies the clouds and moisture. By combining two signs or two Trigrams, a Hexagram is produced. From the respective interactions of the eight signs of the Eight Trigrams, the sixty-four signs of the Hexagrams are formed *(fig 6)*.

Confucius edited *Yijing*, a work which spells out the hidden meaning of the ancient symbols and is used by fortune tellers for divinations. *Feng shui*

15

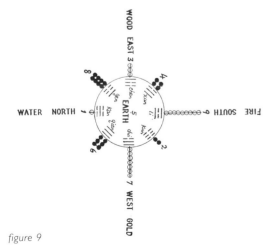

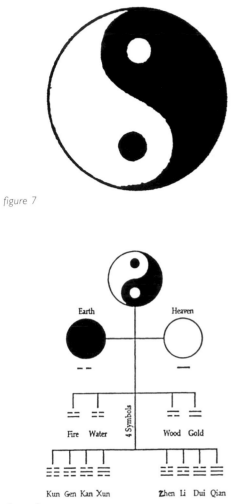

figure 7

Earth   Heaven

Fire Water   4 Symbols   Wood Gold

Kun Gen Kan Xun   Zhen Li Dui Qian

figure 8

figure 9

theory is indirectly related to the *yijing* in the sense that the Eight Trigrams are used to denote the directions. The word *yi* represents the changing nature of all things and the interaction and relation of the *yin* and *yang* qualities of matter in nature. *Jing* means classic, thus the *yijing* has been used as a classical reference for those seeking guidance and an improved quality of life in a technological world. The system used for modern computer programming is based upon the ancient numerals of *yin* and *yang* forming the sixty-four Hexagrams which in turn form a binary coding.

Traditionally, the Eight Trigrams are Chinese systems of arrangements, namely the Former Heaven and the Later Heaven Arrangements. The diagram showing the relationship of the *Minggua*, the Five Elements, the Directions and the Eight Trigrams of the Later Heaven Arrangement can be seen on page 14.

In this technological age, how should man practise *feng shui*? Consultancy work requires the geomancer to apply his or her knowledge of science, architecture and the rudiments of *feng shui* to produce a harmonious union of the tangible and intangible aspects of architecture and *feng shui*. The discipline is so deeply rooted in Chinese architecture that its principles and rudiments were applied to imperial palaces and important buildings throughout the last few dynasties and kingdoms of China. For example, the imperial palaces· in the Forbidden City (*Gugong*) of Beijing were built entirely based on the traditional concepts of *feng shui*. In my book *Feng Shui, The Environments of Power, A Study of Chinese Architecture* the principles of Chinese Architecture, complete with the assessments and analysis of the *feng shui* of the Forbidden City of Beijing, are presented.

The theory of *yin* and *yang* is explained in the texts of *Daodi Jing* (classics of the Dao). The *yin* and *yang* elements are expressed as the dual components that make up the *Taiji* (Extremity and Infinity), the symbol of perfect balance and harmony *(fig 7)*.

The Taiji duality refers to the *yang* sign of *tian* (the heavens) and the *yin di* (the earth). From these, the Five Elements (Gold, Wood, Water, Fire and Earth) are produced. Associated with the Elements are the Eight Trigrams as shown *(figs 8 & 9)*.

The precepts of *yin* and *yang* are contained in the Jin dynasty work, *Zhuanjing* (the classics for burial), by Guo Pu. This classic work states that the good energy of the earth is retained by water but dispersed by wild wind. Many other classics such as the *Qingnang Haijiaojing* and the *Guanshi Dili Zhimong* also present the meaning of *yin* and *yang*. The former states that the hills and rivers represent the energy of the earth. There is *yin* and *yang* in everything. When there is more *yin* than *yang*, it is classified as *yin*;

when more *yang* than *yin*, it is considered *yang*. However, a hill and a source of water can be either *yin* or *yang*, although generally a hill is *yin* and water, *yang*. Thus, there is balance in nature where there is hill and water. A high hill is *yin* while flat land, *yang*. However, when anything is too *yin* it becomes *yang* and vice versa. For example, when the day reaches midday it becomes too *yang* and it turns towards *yin*, and when night reaches midnight it is too *yin* and turns *yang*, becoming day once more.

To achieve a balance of *yin*, *yang* and the Five Elements in the built and natural environments is central to *feng shui* precepts. In the physical and the natural worlds, all things must be in balance and harmony to benefit man. Therefore, the positioning of buildings, the siting of trees and man-made elements, doors and furniture must be well thought out to channel good energy into the interior of the building. *Yin* and *yang* colours must also be used to bring about balance and contrast. Elevational treatment may be made more interesting by the contrast of *yin* and *yang* elements or a certain colour scheme, such as that shown on the elevation of the Federal Reserve Bank of Minneapolis, Minnesota *(fig 10)*.

figure 10

THE LUOSHU AND THE TRIGRAMS

The legendary emperor of China, Fuxi, saw a mythical animal on the Huanghe (the Yellow River) and noted that it was covered with fifty-five black and white dots. This diagram was recorded and named the *Hetu*. Later, the first emperor of the Xia dynasty (2140-1711BC), Dayu, also saw dots forming a similar pattern when he was building outlets to discharge the flood waters of the Huanghe. He finally succeeded in controlling the floods at the end of the thirteenth year. It is said that he saw black (*yin*) and white (*yang*) dots on the back of a huge tortoise (the tortoise had always been associated with divination as attested by the oracle bones – tortoise shells – dating back to 1300BC). From the dots on the tortoise, the diagram of *Hetu* was created. These dots were later translated into Trigrams by Wen Wang of the Zhou dynasty (1231-1135BC). When the *yin* and *yang* dots and the Trigrams were drawn to relate to the Eight Directions and the Five Elements, a diagram called the *Leshu Tu* (the Drawings of the Book of Luo) was formed as shown *(fig 11)*.

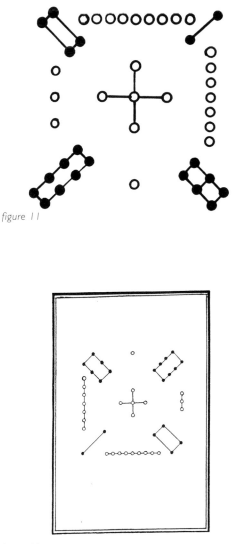
figure 11

This diagram is informative as it illustrates the *yang*/odd numbers one, three, five, seven and nine which are associated with the *tiandao* (the heavens), while the *yin*/even numbers two, four, six and eight are related to the *didao* (the earth). South, being of Fire Element, is the most extreme *yang* element associated with the number nine, which has been used in the design of imperial palaces since ancient times. Another source related that

figure 12

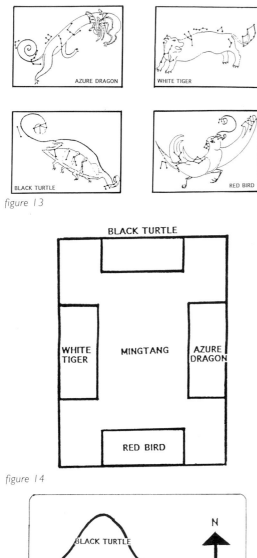

figure 13

figure 14

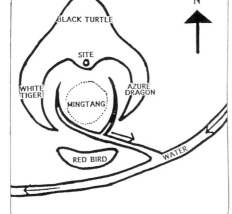

figure 15

Fuxi discovered the relationship between the processes of earthly and cosmic happenings, and drew two diagrams, the *Hetu* and the *Luoshu*, based on his observations. The *Hetu* consisted of fifty-five dots with the numbers one to ten and the *Luoshu*, forty-five dots with the numbers one to nine, the black being *yin* and the white, *yang* (fig **12**).

The celestial sphere was considered to consist of twenty-eight asterisms, which in turn were divided into four heavenly quadrants: the Black Turtle (north), the Azure Dragon (east), the White Tiger (west) and the Red Bird (south) *(figs **13-15**)*. The quadrant positions are analogous with the earthly *feng shui* models.

QI, HILLS AND WATER

Qi, the energy of the earth, exists in the land and can be detected as undulating hills and land forms. It is closely linked with the *li* (shape of land). The theory of *liqi* (the energy of the earth as expressed by the form) has been discussed in Song dynasty writing by the philosopher Zhu Xi (1130-1200) in his *Wenji* (literature). Classical works, such as the *Shanhai Guan* (the Pass of Shanhai) and the *Kaogong Ji* (the Records of the Arts), state the *feng shui* situation of hilly sites. The hilly topography of land form spells the *longmo* (dragon vein) or the *qi* (energy) of the earth. In China it is recognised that the Kunlun Shan is the most powerful range of mountains, consisting of five individual ranges, three of which are in China. These three notable dragons spread from north to south. The north range backs onto the Huanghe, the central enhances the waters of Changjiang, while the southern range spreads across the provinces of Yunnan, Guizhou, Guangxi, Guangzhou, Hunan, Fujian and Zhijiang. One example of a powerful landscape is the Great Wall of China just outside Beijing at the Shanhai Guan in the province of Heibei. Famous *feng shui* mountains in China include the Hengshan, the Huashan, the Taishan and the Lushan (which is most imposing and noted for its breathtaking views and rejuvenating *qi*). The most desirable situation is *fuyin baoyang*, *beishan mianshui* (there is *yin* and *yang*, the rear hills and the front water).

It has been established that a good *feng shui* site must have the *yin* and the *yang* elements, the hill and water and *diqi* (earthly energy) and *shengqi* (heavenly energy). Most of the world's great cities are situated either on hilly sites, have a mountain range as a backdrop or are by the sea or on the banks of beneficial rivers *(figs **16-18**)*. Australian cities are no exception: for example, Sydney, Perth, Brisbane, Melbourne and Adelaide are all sited on such locations *(fig **17**)*.

Water is a beneficial feature because it retains *qi*, while very strong wind is not welcome as it disperses *qi*. Although rivers and seas are sources of *qi*, if they are too shallow or their flow too forceful, they could be destructive. Rivers that tend to flood their banks should be noted and moderated or controlled by engineering works. The Wanghe (the Yellow River), for example, was known in ancient times to cause floods and calamities; it was regarded as a poor *feng shui* element until Dayu channelled away its waters to reduce excessive *qi* (energy). As a river exerts influence on the buildings on its bank, the relationship between the flow of the river and the siting of buildings may be favourable or unfavourable.

The geomancer classifies water according to the following conditions: rivers must be long and winding; the flow of water must pass by the front of a building; sea water must be deep *(fig 19)*; lake water must be calm *(fig 20)*; pond water must be clear. On the other hand, water that causes *shaqi* flows rapidly. It is therefore inauspicious when it dries up in autumn and winter or in times of dry weather. It is also undesirable when it stagnates and produces a bad smell.

Qi comes in many forms. There is *shengqi* (vibrant energy) and *siqi* (stifling energy); *yangqi* (sun energy) and *yinqi* (moon energy); *tuqi* (energy from the ground) and *diqi* (earth energy); *chengqi* (moving energy) and *juqi* (conjoining energy). *Qi* can also be classified as being heavenly, earthly and human. Heavenly *qi* is related to astronomy, cyclical timing, climatic and seasonal changes, as well as the natural forces such as wind and rain. Earthly *qi* is that related to the earth's topography and magnetic forces, earthly features such as the natural and built forms in the environment, space and structure, colours and lighting. Human *qi* can be equated to political, cultural and social influences.

Personal disposition, habit, nature and sensitivity of a person may be classified as humanly *qi*. The Chinese saying *qi shi wan mu zhi yuan* (qi is the source of all things) echoes another saying *qi xing ce shui chu, shui zhi ceqi zhi* which means that when there is *qi*, water flows, but when water stops flowing, *qi* has been exhausted. It is of vital importance that the important areas of living and working are located at the *qi* areas. This must have been why the ancients usually had a geomancer determine the position of *shengqi* for *dongtu* (the starting of construction) on a building site.

FENG SHUI INSTRUMENTS

In Confucius classics, such as the *Shijing* and the *Shujing* diagrams, geomancers are shown examining the ground conditions with instruments that resemble the modern-day geomancer compass, the *luopan*. As early as the Han dynasty (206BC–AD220), *luopans* were made relating to the Directions,

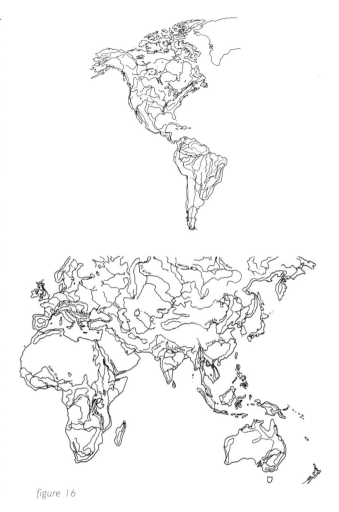

figure 16

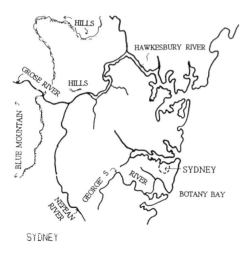

SYDNEY

BRISBANE

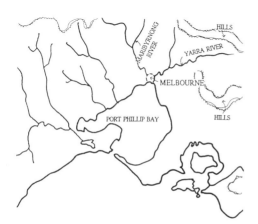

MELBOURNE

figure 17

with reference to the twenty-eight Asterisms or Constellations, namely *jiao wu jiao, kang jin long, si tu he, fang ren tu, xin yue lang, wei huo hu, qi shui pao, dou mu xie, niu jin niu, nu tu fu, xu ren su, wei yue yan, shi huo ju, pi shui yu, kui mu lang, lou jin gou, wei tu zhi, yang ren ji, pi yue liao, zi huo hou, shen shui hou, jin wu han, kui jin yang, liu tu zhang, xin ren ma, zhang yue lu, yi huo she* and *zhen shui yin.* These *luopans* were used to locate the *qi* of the earth. As the Constellations are closely related to the Five Elements, they are believed to exert influence on man's daily activities according to his Element.

There are two schools of *feng shui*: one makes use of instruments and methods of calculation, while the other depends on assessment of land form and acquired experience. For the former, the *luopan* is an important *feng shui* instrument for finding the direction and orientation of a building, the *qi* location and the relationship of the orientation with the stars. The first Han *luopan* consisted of a magnetic spoon on a diviner's board. This diviner's board was developed and it slowly evolved to the present form with a magnetic needle in the centre and a turntable of many rings of information radiating from the centre.

Early *luopans* were simply designed containing twenty-four directions derived from the Ten Heavenly Stems and the Twelve Earthly Branches in the Later Heaven Arrangement. A modern-day *luopan*, containing the *tianpan* (heaven's pool), the *dipan* (earth's pool) and the *renpan* (man's pool), is mounted on a red board *(fig 21)*. Its central ring, the heaven pool, contains a south-pointing magnetic needle. In the pools of heaven, earth and man, twenty-four directions are marked using the names of the Heavenly Stems, Earthly Branches and Trigrams. The *tianpan* is used to detect locations with reference to water courses; the *dipan* is used to locate the *qi* (commonly known as the dragon) of the site; and the *renpan* is used to assess the topography of land.

There are many variations in the design of a *luopan*. Each manufacturer may make it differently from the other, thus each type is read with particular reference to the maker's instruction manual. However, in reading the *luopan*, the following points must be considered: the first ring usually refers to the Eight Trigrams (*Qian, Kun, Zhen, Kan, Gen, Xun, Li* and *Dui*) which reflect the cosmic movements of the universe. The Trigrams and eight directions are used to assess the course of underground water courses.

The second ring of some *luopans* refer to the Later Heaven Trigrams. This ring may be compared with the first to find out if there is balance in terms of *yin/yang*. If the facade of the building is too *yin*, a change of colour scheme to a warmer tone may make it more balanced. On the other hand, if it is too *yang*, the colour may be made more *yin*. The rings that follow may be used to find the favourable locations and orientations of the building.

To assess the *qi* of the earth and to determine the portents of the twenty-four stars, the *Ershi Silu* (the twenty-four directions) are assessed. The twenty-four directions are: *wu* (south), *ding, wei, kun, shen, geng, you* (west), *xin, shu, qian, hai, ren, zi* (north), *kui, chou, gen, yin, zia, mao* (east), *yi, chen, xun, si* and *bing*. The twenty-four directions are aligned with the positions of the Nine Stars so that they are in harmony and in a productive order. For example, *tanlang* (Wood Element) should be in the direction of *gen* (Wood Element) and *bing* (Fire Element); Wood is in a productive order with Fire, therefore the association with *tanlang, gen* and *bing*, is auspicious. The water courses are assessed by making reference to the Nine Stars. Favourable water courses are those that flow in the direction of the *tanlang, wujue, juemen, yupi* and *luchuan*. The last ring of the compass is usually on the twenty-eight Asterisms.

When using the *luopan* care must be taken not to distort the reading by avoiding the following: placing magnetic equipment or objects near the instrument; placing the *luopan* near reinforced beams or columns; and reading the *luopan* near metallic objects. If necessary, the reading can be crosschecked with the reading of another compass. In assessing the dimensions of doors and furniture, a geomancer's ruler is used *(fig 21)*. This ruler is called the *lupanchi* (the ruler of *luopan*) as it is believed to have been created by the well-known craftsman, Lu Pan, in the Lu State of the Chunqiu era (722BC-AD481). This *feng shui* ruler contains eight divisions, some of which are auspicious, others, not. Some auspicious dimensions are as follows: doors – 86, 88, 107cm (main doors, 108, 125cm); corridors – 108 or 146cm; ceilings – 300, 320cm; room width – 300, 320, 368, 390, 408, 428, 448, 468, 495cm. For the measurement of the main door and the more important furniture, such as the table used by the Managing Director, the geomancer's ruler or measuring tape should be used.

figure 18

figure 19

figure 20

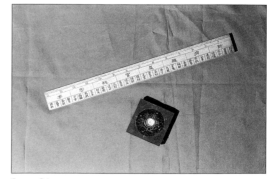
figure 21

PART TWO

HOW TO ASSESS *FENG SHUI*

FENG SHUI GARDENS AND LANDSCAPE

Before presenting my assessment of *feng shui*, design considerations such as landscaping, planning and interior design should be discussed.

Chinese landscape design is unique and very different from Western garden design; the underlying concept is based on intuition and freedom. Unlike the formal and systematic approach of the garden in the West, Chinese garden design is based on the *feng shui* precepts of harmony and the contrast of *yin* and *yang*. A *feng shui* landscape garden is like a Chinese brush painting: there must be *yang* elements – such as rocks, hills or *shan* – and *yin* elements – such as water or *shui*, covered and uncovered space, built-up areas and courtyards, covered walkways and exposed paths, arched bridges and zigzagged links, tall structures such as pagodas and low-rise or single-storey pavilions. A landscaped garden must present a sense of anticipation, peace and tranquillity, in addition to interesting views.

The desired criteria include: contrasting large open spaces and small semi-covered spaces; connecting zigzagging narrow walkways for circulation; the location of pavilions behind rockeries or thick wooded areas; the use of walls and other elements to enclose spaces; creating, grouping or dispersing elements of design; creating rhythm in the design of spaces; creating a sense of light and shade; creating differences in levels of pavements and floors of buildings; creating perspectives and borrowed vistas; and finally, creating a sense of balance and harmony.

However, landscape gardens are incomplete without spaces modelled on Confucian and Daoist ideas. To enhance the spatial concept of a garden, the designer makes use of high and low land, inserts man-made water sources to enhance *qi* and introduces rockeries and plants to create harmony and balance. Landscape gardens are created to express *chang* (hidden) and *lu* (exposed) as well as *she* (void) and *shi* (solid) areas. The planting of trees or the location of ponds, rocks and bridges is carried out with reference to the Element of the position of the site. For example, the north and northwest may be used to site ponds, pools or water features, and willow trees are best positioned along the side of a pond. Rockeries should provide a backdrop to the setting and contrast to the pond, while *yin* trees are best located in the north, with *yang* trees to the south. Bridges link *qi* and should be curved, arched or zigzagged to reduce *shaqi*.

FENG SHUI FORM AND PLANNING

It is important to capture the good *qi* of a site for the benefit of man; however, it is also vital to mould the form, shape and space of man's dwelling and place of work. Thus, the site, the surrounding environment, the interior environment, the planning, the design and finish of man's shelter are equally important in the assessment of *feng shui*. In the Qing dynasty writing, *Gujin Tushu Jicheng* (section 670), the importance of the above is implied. The Chinese have long since established a model *feng shui* situation: for example, in a situation where the north wind is cold, not only is it best to have a hill at the rear and north, and a lake in front, but also to have the ground to the left higher than that to the right.

The *qi* of a place is intuitive and intangible as it cannot be seen. However, the *xue* or form (primitive dwelling/cave) is physical and tangible as it can be seen and designed. The *qi* is the empty and the void, while the *xue* is the built-up part of a place or complex. For example, in a Chinese traditional house, the *qi* is equated with the *mingtang* (the courtyard) while the *xue* is the built-up or interior space of the *zhai* (house). An ideal burial place and ideal living quarters are principally similar in planning – both are supposed to have a *mingtang* and a built-up *xue*. The relationship of this *xue* with the surrounding landscape and Elements is of importance to the *feng shui* of the *xue*. The main entrance to this *xue* is also of importance, as mentioned in the *Gujin Tushu Jicheng*.

FENG SHUI COLOUR AND INTERIOR DESIGN

As shown on page 15, colours can be classified under the Five Elements. Colours are also classified as either *yin* or *yang*. Generally, all cool colours

Figure 23 – The elevational treatment of Queen Square, Bath, designed by John Wood the Elder, is made up of shapes of Fire and Wood Elements.

CASE STUDIES OF *FENG SHUI* FORM AND SHAPE

The form and shape of a space, a structure or a building element can be listed or classified under the Five paired Elements as follows: water (intuitive zigzag shape) with wood (elongated/rectangular); wood with fire (triangular); fire with earth (square); earth with gold (round); gold with water (free form). Various buildings of differing Element, plan or elevational treatment are illustrated below.

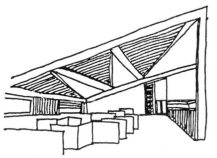

figure 24

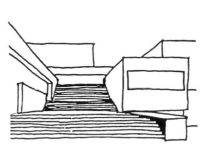

figure 25

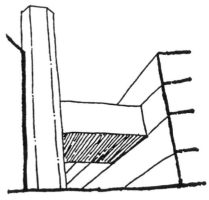

figure 26

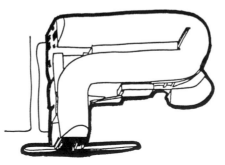

figure 27

Figures 24-27 The combination of various forms and shapes of a building complex should be made with reference to the Element of the form or shape. Examples of auspicious and inauspicious combinations can be seen: fig 24 – auspicious combination of triangular (fire) and square (earth) shapes; fig 25 – inauspicious combination of rectangular (wood) and square (earth) shapes; fig 26 – neutral (wood with wood); fig 27 – auspicious intuitive (water) and rectangular (wood) shapes.

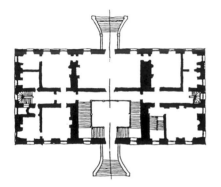

figure 28

Figure 28 – The spatial forms and elevational shapes of Coleshill, Berkshire, are of Wood and Earth Elements.

figure 29

Figure 29 – The external elements of St Paul's Cathedral, London, are also made up of shapes of many Elements such as Gold, Fire, Wood and Earth. On the other hand, the plan is made up of spatial forms of mainly Gold and Earth.

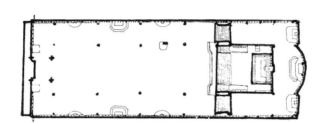

figure 30

Figure 30 – Le Raincy Notre Dame was also designed in plan as Wood Element, and in perspective its Wood Element is complemented by the Fire Element.

figure 31

Figure 31 – The compatible Elements of shape, Wood and Fire, are often used for bridge design. The Salginatobel Bridge, Switzerland, as shown in the drawing on the right by Robert Maillart provides a good example.

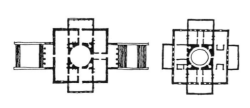

figure 32

Figure 32 – Mereworth, Kent, has a central space of Gold Element and an outer interior space of Earth Element. Earth produces Gold and so the Elements are in harmony.

FROM ABOVE: Figure 33 – The interior of St Stephen Walbrook, London, displays mainly spatial volumes and Elements of Gold and Wood; Figure 34 – The interior of St Martin-in-the-Fields, London, is enhanced by the contrast of various shapes and forms of Gold and Wood.

are *yin* and all warm colours, *yang*. The balance of *yin* and *yang* and the use of favourable colours according to the Element of the user of the space is important in the design of an interior. The colour scheme introduced must enhance the balance of the interior and the contrast of the exterior. Because he deals with space, form and structure, an expert in *feng shui* should also be a sensitive interior designer. His sensitivity and awareness of the built interior helps him to reorganise a poor *feng shui* design. In planning a *feng shui* interior, the expert should be fully conscious of what he sees from all possible angles within the confines of the interior space. For renovation work, he has to detect the defects of the interior in terms of *feng shui* and other design considerations which affect the wellbeing of the occupants. The composition of form and space, colour scheme and pattern and texture, for example, affect *feng shui* in many ways.

THE ASSESSMENT OF THE *FENG SHUI* OF A BUILDING

Although there are several ways of assessing the *feng shui* of a building (some based on method and calculation, others through studying land form, detecting water courses, and locating important areas in the *qi* points), the modern geomancer makes use of all available knowledge and examines the building with reference to every method with which he is familiar. If the assessment is made on an existing building, it includes the examination of the site and assessment of the relationship of the existing building with its surrounding physical and built environment; studying the topography of the land; noting the favourable and unfavourable features of the aforementioned; and analysing the birth date of the owner/user and his/her Element of Birth.

Another method refers to the *Minggua* and the *Feixing* Magic Diagrams. Once the basic analysis has been made, a diagram of location can be sketched. Once the favourable locations are determined, the existing or proposed building is checked and recommendations made. However, it must be made clear that the location of the various built-up areas is only one aspect of the assessment. The other equally important factors to consider are the *yun* (era) during which the building was built, site topography, landscape and other physical features on site. These aspects are, of course, best analysed by skilled geomancers – the more skilful the geomancer is in terms of site planning and design, the better the *feng shui*.

If the assessment is made on a proposed building, the site must be studied in addition to the physical environment surrounding the site. For example, in Beijing, where the cold wind and dust come from the north, it is best to orientate windows to the south and the lake *(fig 35)*.

The owners' *Minggua* must be considered in the reorganisation of the building; several case studies will be presented in the following chapter. For complicated proposed building complexes, the best geomancers are those trained in architectural design or engineering; experience in handling sizable projects is essential. According to the *Minggua* method, the locations of the important areas such as the main door, the master bedroom and the kitchen of a house are determined by the compatibility of the Element of the *gua* and the direction or location. For example, the east (*Zhen* of Wood) direction is good for the *Kangua*, which is north and of Water Element. The southwest (*Kun* of Earth) direction is compatible for the *Qiangua* (northwest and Gold) and the *Duigua* (west and Gold). The east (*Zhen* of Wood) and southeast (*Xun* of Wood) directions are in harmony with the *Ligua* (south and Fire). The north (*Kan* of Water) is good for the *Zhengua* (east and Wood) and the *Xungua* (southwest and Wood). The south is auspicious for the *Gengua* (northeast and Earth).

In contrast, the southwest is not good for the *Kangua* (north and Water). The northwest or the west are not auspicious for the *Zhengua* (east and Wood) or the *Xungua* (southeast and Wood). The south is not in harmony with the *Qiangua* (northwest and Gold) or the *Duigua* (west and Gold). The east or the southeast is not compatible with the *Gengua* (northeast and Earth) or the *Kungua* (southwest and Earth). The northwest is not good for the *Ligua* (south and Fire). The compatibility and incompatibility of *gua* and directions may be summarised in the charts as shown in the chart on page 28 (those not listed are average locations). These charts can only be used as a guide. A detailed assessment of *feng shui* involves a more comprehensive analysis of the horoscopic characteristics of the occupants of the buildings and a complete analysis of the sites and their surroundings.

figure 35

YEAR OF BIRTH	GUA OR TRIGRAM		YEAR OF BIRTH	GUA OR TRIGRAM	
	MALE	FEMALE		MALE	FEMALE
1930	DUI	GEN	1972	KAN	GEN
1931	QIAN	LI	1973	LI	QIAN
1932	KUN	KAN	1974	GEN	DUI
1933	XUN	KUN	1975	DUI	GEN
1934	ZHEN	ZHEN	1976	QIAN	LI
1935	KUN	XUN	1977	KUN	KAN
1936	KAN	GEN	1978	XUN	KUN
1937	LI	QIAN	1979	ZHEN	ZHEN
1938	GEN	DUI	1980	KUN	XUN
1939	DUI	GEN	1981	KAN	GEN
1940	QIAN	LI	1982	LI	QIAN
1941	KUN	KAN	1983	GEN	DUI
1942	XUN	KUN	1984	DUI	GEN
1943	ZHEN	ZHEN	1985	QIAN	LI
1944	KUN	XUN	1986	KUN	KAN
1945	KAN	GEN	1987	XUN	KUN
1946	LI	QIAN	1988	ZHEN	ZHEN
1947	GEN	DUI	1989	KUN	XUN
1948	DUI	GEN	1990	KAN	GEN
1949	QIAN	LI	1991	LI	QIAN
1950	KUN	KAN	1992	GEN	DUI
1951	XUN	KUN	1993	DUI	GEN
1952	ZHEN	ZHEN	1994	QIAN	LI
1953	KUN	GEN	1995	KUN	KAN
1954	KAN	KUN	1996	XUN	KUN
1955	LI	QIAN	1997	ZHEN	ZHEN
1956	GEN	DUI	1998	KUN	GEN
1957	DUI	GEN	1999	KAN	KUN
1958	QIAN	LI	2000	LI	QIAN
1959	KUN	KAN	2001	GEN	DUI
1960	XUN	KUN	2002	DUI	GEN
1961	CHEN	CHEN	2003	QIAN	LI
1962	KUN	XUN	2004	KUN	KAN
1963	KAN	GEN	2005	XUN	KUN
1964	LI	QIAN	2006	CHEN	CHEN
1965	GEN	DUI	2007	KUN	XUN
1966	DUI	GEN	2008	KAN	GEN
1967	QIAN	LI	2009	LI	QIAN
1968	KUN	KAN	2010	GEN	DUI
1969	XUN	KUN			
1970	ZHEN	ZHEN			
1971	KUN	XUN			

figure 36

CASE STUDIES OF COMMERCIAL BUILDINGS

Before a commercial project is designed and implemented, a thorough market analysis must be made. The feasibility study, the choice of a suitable site, the selection of an appropriate brief and the identification of prospective clients are important considerations and are all part and parcel of the project's *feng shui* considerations. In addition, site location, accessibility to the site, internal and external circulation, planning and design, and the relationship between the commercial project and other complexes are prime factors indicative of a project's success or failure. For example, the original design and planning of Foster's Hongkong and Shanghai Bank (*fig 38*) was subjected to changes suggested by the geomancer, and circulation routes and structural elements were changed for better *feng shui*.

LOCATIONS OF MAIN AREAS
(N = NORTH, NE = NORTHEAST, E = EAST, SE = SOUTHEAST, S = SOUTH, SW = SOUTHWEST, W = WEST, NW = NORTHWEST)

QIANGUA OF GOLD ELEMENT

FAVOURABLE	UNFAVOURABLE
SW, W, NW	N, E, SE, S

KANGUA OF WATER ELEMENT

FAVOURABLE	UNFAVOURABLE
SE, E,	SW, NW, W

GENGUA OF EARTH ELEMENT

FAVOURABLE	UNFAVOURABLE
SW, W, NW	N, E, SE,

ZHENGUA OF WOOD ELEMENT

FAVOURABLE	UNFAVOURABLE
SE, S, N, E	SW, W, NW

XUNGUA OF WOOD ELEMENT

FAVOURABLE	UNFAVOURABLE
E, SE	SW, W, NW

LIGUA OF FIRE ELEMENT

FAVOURABLE	UNFAVOURABLE
SE, S	SW, W, NW

KUNGUA OF EARTH ELEMENT

FAVOURABLE	UNFAVOURABLE
SW, S, NW	N, E, SE,

DUIGUA OF GOLD ELEMENT

FAVOURABLE	UNFAVOURABLE
NW, SW	N, E, SE, S

figure 37

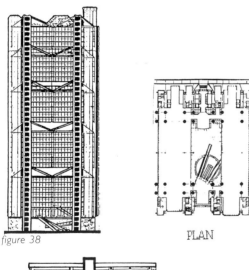

figure 38

PLAN

figure 39

The location of the main door of a commercial building can be assessed and decided by the *Minggua* method or other methods mentioned in the previous chapters. It can also be determined by the study of the geographical and environmental factors. In most cases, all factors affecting the project must be taken into consideration in the placement of the main entrance.

The planning, structure and aesthetics of the building are equally influential factors. Good planning should facilitate efficient circulation, ventilation and harmonious natural and artificial lighting. It is also important to ensure that the architectural treatment of commercial building complexes is unified. The site should allow for loading and unloading service facilities, disposal of rubbish and customer parking. The possibility of future extensions must also be taken into account. If the project is a mixed residential and commercial development, functional and physical integration of different components of the project should be provided. Pedestrian routes should be one of the first planning considerations.

The interior design of a commercial building should reflect balance and harmony in terms of placing various design elements, the implementation of colour schemes, the application of textured materials and the installation of the various mechanical, ventilation and lighting schemes. It is advantageous to design and build collapsable partitions in commercial buildings to allow for changes in tenancy. In shopping centres, circulation routes must be carefully planned to allow maximum exposure to the shops. The use of interesting and attractive signs may provide a refreshing atmosphere within the centre, while multi-level volumes within a centre enhance the *qi* and interest of the interior. Lighting should be designed to complement rather than detract from the shop signs. The symbolism of words used in the signs must be auspicious as the following examples demonstrate: 'Jinjin Woodworks' (*jin* means gold, which cuts wood); 'Huoshan Goldsmith' (*huo* means fire which melts gold); 'Qingshui Woodworks' (*qingshui* means clear water which nourishes wood); 'Dadi Goldsmith' (*dadi* means huge earth which produces gold) Logos used for company trademarks and signs must be well conceived. The Elements of geometry must be studied and the combination of shapes for the logos must be devised auspiciously. For example, a triangle should not be combined with a circle because fire (triangle) melts gold (circle).

Seen in section, the commercial building *(fig 39)* is fortuitously sited with the entrance facing the lower ground and the rear portion facing the hill. Efficient drainage is provided by a deep surface drain just below the hill. The foundations are structurally sound and proper tanking has been provided on the retaining wall.

Figure **40** shows the section of a commercial building with the rear of the building facing the lower ground. The building is triangular, as if half of the word *jin* (Gold) has been cut off. This bodes ill. Another commercial building *(fig* **41***)* looks simple in section. However, standing eighteen storeys high, it could have more than one level below ground and the lower floor heights could be more generous. As it is, the *qi* of the ground level is stifled as the ceiling height is too low.

Figure **42** shows a shopping centre which is successful because it has ample car parking, and its internal pedestrian area allows shoppers to feel relaxed and at the same time enjoy good views of the shops on both sides.

Commercial projects such as highrise office blocks must be situated on prominent sites with easy access for pedestrians and vehicles, and close to a rapid transit transport system and public facilities such as food and shopping centres. The planning of an office floor should be equally flexible to allow for subletting.

Figure **43** shows an example of a spacious office lift lobby of a large office floor which has been sublet to two other tenants. The lobby accommodates a reception area which helps to direct clients and visitors to the various offices in an efficient manner. Placement of logos and signboards should be made with reference to the *Minggua* of the owner and director of the company. Offices should be planned to allow executives to circulate with ease via an interconnecting communication network. Narrow corridors and the awkward placement of office doors should be avoided.

In the event of fire, an efficient means of escape is of paramount importance. Artificial plants or ornamental objects should not obstruct passages to fire escapes or staircases *(fig* **44***)*. The distance from the remotest corner of the office to the fire escape should meet with local authority building regulations, but not be too near, which is uneconomical *(fig* **45** A and B) nor too far (C). Toilets, meanwhile, should not be placed in the north, nor should the doors to the female and male toilets be located too near to one another *(fig* **46***)*. It is good practice to place a store or utility room between the toilets.

The location of the chief executive's office should be chosen with reference to his *Minggua*. The room should be relatively spacious and appropriately furnished. Door, desks and chairs should be placed in accordance with *feng shui* rules – for example, the executive's chair should be placed against a solid wall rather than a glass wall. The lighting, acoustics and ambience of a conference room should encourage harmonious dialogue, and the chairman of a meeting in the conference room should be placed in front of a solid wall *(fig* **47***)*. In addition to ensuring that the building

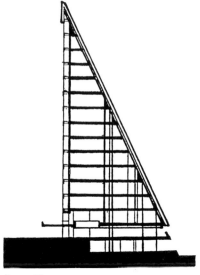
figure 40

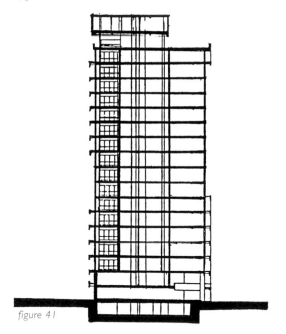
figure 41

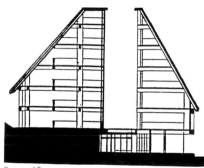
figure 42

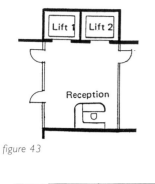

figure 43

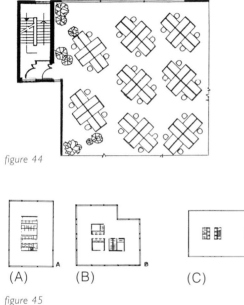

figure 44

(A) (B) (C)

figure 45

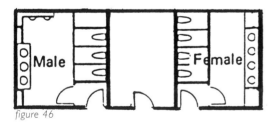

Male   Female

figure 46

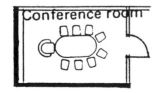

Conference room

figure 47

design and planning conform to *feng shui* rules, it is important to ensure that proper security devices such as fire and alarm systems are installed.

Although developers do not necessarily take *feng shui* considerations into account, potential occupants of an office block or commercial building are becoming increasingly sensitive to *feng shui* and environmental needs. The intangible aspects of a building can no longer be overlooked.

CASE STUDIES OF PUBLIC BUILDINGS

The art of siting a public building is similar to that of any other building type. As with commercial developments, the entire site and surrounding environment must be explored and studied carefully before the buildings are located. The geological nature and the formation of the land, topographical features and the existing vegetation of the site, as well as the surrounding areas, must be assessed before decisions regarding the type of foundation, structural framework and placement of the structure can be made. Buildings should not be sited on areas where there is evidence of settlement, moisture or thermal movement.

In the design of large public buildings, such as hospitals, the following should be carefully considered: the entrances (main, staff, emergency and service) must be well placed to facilitate efficiency, and the reception must be immediately apparent; circulation patterns must be clear to flow efficiently; siting should be in accordance with the rules of *feng shui*; the building must be accessible by foot, bus and car; sufficient parking facilities must be provided; and provision must also be made to accommodate future expansion and changes in the *feng shui* cycle.

The efficient use of rooms must be planned appropriately. For example, in a hospital the mortuary (being a *yin* area) should not be next to the restaurant (*yang*). *Figure 48* shows a poor example of planning which was then changed to create better *feng shui*. The mortuary was originally next to the pharmacy; patients disliked such an arrangement and so the layout was altered to improve *feng shui*. The original plan of the hospital had one entrance for outpatients and emergency cases. Much confusion was created and eventually another entrance was added to ease the pressure of circulation. The alteration also improved the *qi* of the entrance according to the *Feixing* Magic Diagram *(fig 50)*.

Other public buildings, such as museums and art galleries, may be subjected to *feng shui* assessment less frequently because these buildings are either government or corporate owned and are not sold or leased to business investors. However, it is important to consider the following: location of site in relation to other buildings; external shape and internal space;

structure and cladding; flexibility and feasibility; and lighting and mechanical items. The location of the site should be free from the ill effects of *feng shui*. External shape should be in harmony with the surrounding built forms, and internal space should allow for clarity of circulation *(fig 49)*. Confused circulation is problematic.

The structure of a building should be adequately designed. Whenever possible, freestanding columns should be round. The cladding should shield the interior from glare without being too reflective. Interior space should allow for great flexibility of displayed artwork. Special lighting may be required; artificial lighting can create a satisfying ambience as well as enhancing the exhibits. Frank Lloyd Wright's Guggenheim Museum in New York is a fine example of an art museum of Gold Element, based on an interesting spatial concept *(fig 51)*.

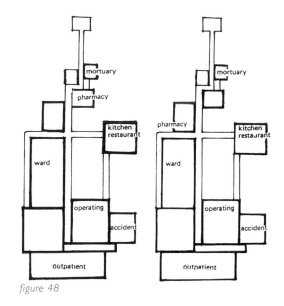

figure 48

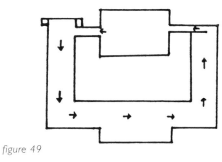

figure 49

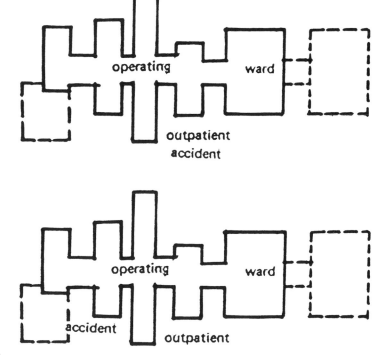

figure 50

31

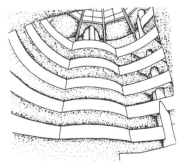

figure 51

figure 52

Religious buildings and temples can also be classified as public buildings. Most Chinese buildings are sited and designed with reference to the *feng shui* of the site. In Southeast Asia, Chinese temples are based on the concept of balance, symmetry and wall-enclosure, and are often orientated with reference to the precepts of geomancy. Tianfu Gong in Singapore and many others were first sited to face the sea *(fig 52)*. However, in Thailand, many temples are of Fire Element in form *(fig 53)*.

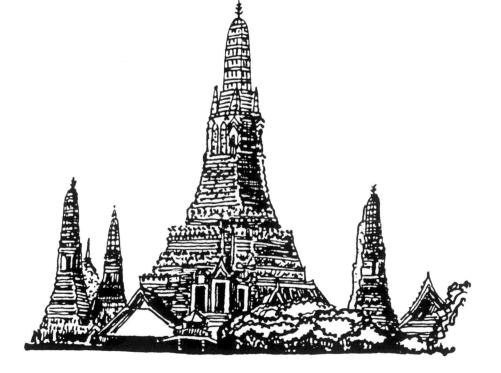

figure 53

CASE STUDIES OF RESIDENTIAL BUILDINGS

Several cases of renovations and improvements of residential buildings are given below with drawings of house plans before (left-hand plans) and after (right-hand plans) renovation to illustrate how defects of *feng shui* can be eliminated.

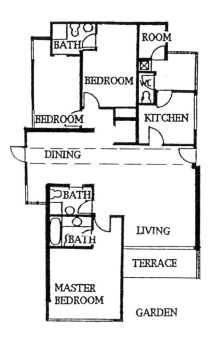
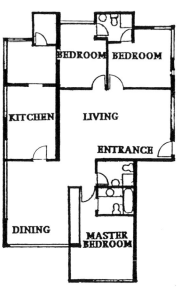
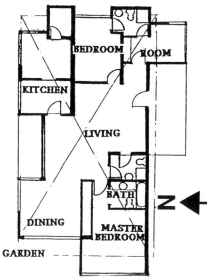
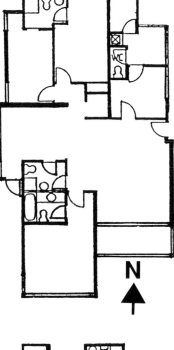

figure 54

Figure 54 – The first case study reveals the defect of 'excessively vibrant qi' through the front and back doors. It is noted that if the front is in alignment with the back door, the qi passes through too quickly and adversely affects the luck of the tenants. Thus, renovation of the doors is required.

Figure 55 – The kitchen in the northeast is too small, as are the dining room and third bedroom. Alterations would improve the feng shui.

figure 55

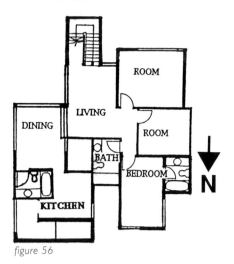

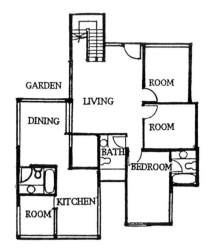

figure 56

Figure 56 – This house has its entrance set back to the south. Even though the approach is pleasant, the living room is too narrow. The kitchen is poorly lit and is therefore too yin. The bathroom is in the north which is not a desirable location. To improve the feng shui, the entrance is pushed out to make a more spacious entrance, allowing qi to flow in. The kitchen is enlarged and more natural light and ventilation is introduced. The living room is also enlarged to allow qi to flow easily.

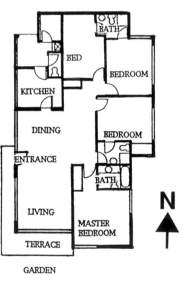

figure 57

Figure 57 – Every space or room should be of an appropriate size or scale in accordance with its importance. The living room should be larger than the dining room. Similarly, the master bedroom should be larger than the guest room. The original plan shows defects of scale and size of rooms.

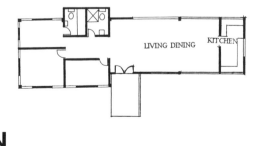

figure 58

Figure 58 – This plan shows a house with a small kitchen and limited dining space. The entrance is set back in a tight space. The kitchen and part of the dining space are covered by a lean-to roof that appears awkward. Irrespective of the Minggua of the owner, this house plan requires improvement. To improve the feng shui, this house was lengthened, the kitchen and the dining areas were shifted to the east, and the entrance pushed out to make the house more wholesome with every space under one roof.

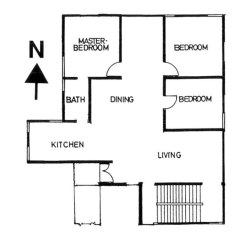

Figure 59 – The entrance to this house originally faced the staircase. Changes could be made to improve the feng shui by relocating the entrance.

figure 59

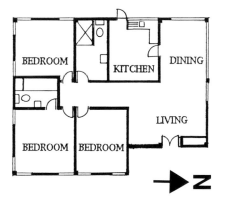

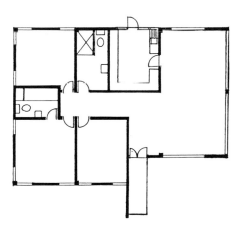

Figure 60 – This house has its entrance set back in the northeast. The living room is too small, hence the it needs to be enlarged to allow qi to flow at ease.

figure 60

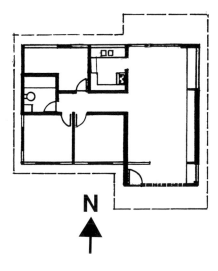

Figure 61 – The entrance door of this house was in line with the rear door. The owner lost a great deal of money and the entrance was simply redesigned by placing a screen in front of the main door as shown below.

figure 61

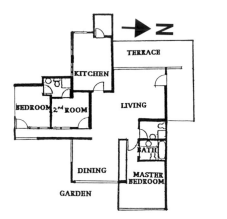
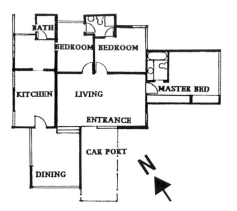

figures 62a & b

Figure 62a – This house has the following feng shui defects: the occupant of the second bedroom is of Water Element and is too near the kitchen (Fire Element) for comfort; ventilation in the second bedroom is poor as it is indirectly ventilated through the window at the end of the corridor; the dining room is too far from the kitchen; and the living room is facing the setting sun. Figure 62b – The living room of this house is too confined and needs to be extended.

figure 63

Figure 63 – The store room of this house spoilt the spatial quality of the living/dining space. The entrance to the east was not suitable for the owner, whose Minggua was Zhenggua. The store room was demolished to make sufficient space for living, dining and cooking. The entrance was moved to the south for better feng shui.

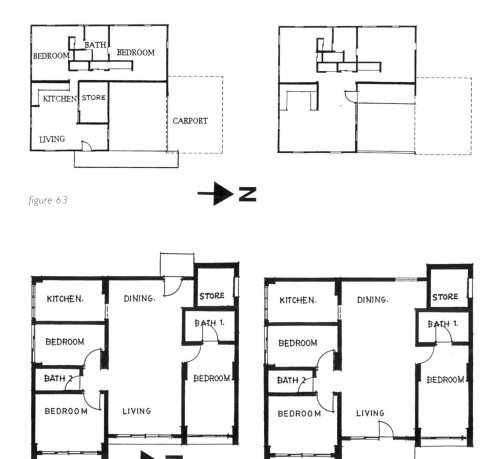

figure 64

Figure 64 – This house was originally orientated to face west as the Minggua of the owner was Genggua. When the owner opened another door facing east and used it as his main entrance he fell ill on account of the inauspicious orientation for people of Genggua.

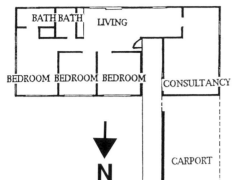
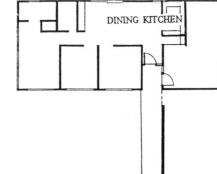

BATH BATH LIVING

DINING KITCHEN

BEDROOM BEDROOM BEDROOM CONSULTANCY

CARPORT

N

figure 65

Figure 65 – These plans show the improvements made to a small consultancy and residential unit for a medical doctor. The entrance to the house in the original plan was too yin. The improved plan brings more qi to the living room.

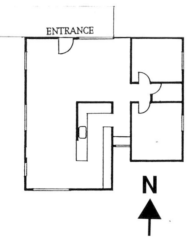
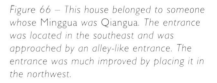

LIVING BEDROOM

BATH

KITCHEN BEDROOM

DINING ENTRANCE

ENTRANCE

N

figure 66

Figure 66 – This house belonged to someone whose Minggua was Qiangua. The entrance was located in the southeast and was approached by an alley-like entrance. The entrance was much improved by placing it in the northwest.

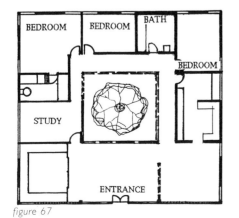
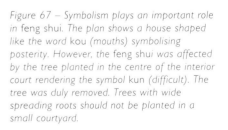

BEDROOM BEDROOM BATH

BEDROOM

STUDY

ENTRANCE

COURTYARD

figure 67

Figure 67 – Symbolism plays an important role in feng shui. The plan shows a house shaped like the word kou (mouths) symbolising posterity. However, the feng shui was affected by the tree planted in the centre of the interior court rendering the symbol kun (difficult). The tree was duly removed. Trees with wide spreading roots should not be planted in a small courtyard.

PART THREE

HOW TO PRACTISE *FENG SHUI*

figure A

SE
3	8	1
2	4	6
7	9	5

S
8	4	6
7	9	2
3	5	1

SW
1	6	8
9	2	4
5	7	3

E
2	7	9
1	3	5
6	8	4

4	9	2
3	5	7
8	1	6

W
6	2	4
5	7	9
1	3	8

NE
7	3	5
6	8	1
2	4	9

N
9	5	7
8	1	3
4	6	2

NW
5	1	3
4	6	8
9	2	7

figure B

SE
3	8	1
2	4	6
7	9	5

S
8	4	6
7	9	2
3	5	1

SW
1	6	8
9	2	4
5	7	3

E
4	8	6
5	3	1
9	7	2

4	9	2
3	5	7
8	1	6

W
8	3	1
9	7	5
4	2	6

NE
7	3	5
6	8	1
2	4	9

N
2	6	4
3	1	8
7	5	9

NW
7	2	9
8	6	4
3	1	5

There are many ways in which to approach *feng shui*, even though they can be divided into two broad categories: the Form School and the Method School. The former is based on the study and assessment of the site's topography and the surrounding natural and built forms; the latter is based on the *Minggua* and horoscopes of the users for the orientation of the buildings. In this section, the Method School is presented.

BAZHAI MINGJIN METHOD OF *FENG SHUI*

There are several ways of assessing the *feng shui* of a place according to the Method School, one of which is based on the *Bazhai Mingjin* method. By this method, people may be classified generally into either the Eastern or the Western Four Houses according to their natal Trigram or their year of birth. This method is fairly similar to the *Minggua* method, and the categorisation relies upon the following premise: Eastern Four Houses (people with *Minggua* of *Li, Kan, Zhen* and *Xun*); Western Four Houses (people with *Minggua* of *Qian, Kun, Gen* and *Dui*).

The *gua* of *Li, Kan, Zhen* and *Xun* are grouped together and between them *Zhen* and *Xun* (both of Wood Element) produce *Li* (Fire Element), *Kan* (Water Element) produces *Zhen* and *Xun* (Wood Element). Similarly, among the Western Trigrams *Qian* and *Dui* are both Gold, and *Gen* and *Kun* are Earth. Earth produces Gold and thus Earth and Gold are productive Elements. Those who belong to the Eastern Houses should not have their entrances, bedrooms or kitchen in the westerly directions. Similarly, those of the Western Houses should not have their entrances, bedrooms and kitchens in the easterly directions.

To locate the living or working spaces, the centre of the building has to be determined. If the shape of the building is a square or a rectangle, the centre of the building can be located easily. However, if the shape of the building is awkward, the centre of the building has to be worked out; if the plan is not available, a measured drawing has to be undertaken.

The natal charts or horoscopes of the users of the building are not the only guidelines for the assessment of the *feng shui* of a place: the topographic features and levels and the man-made and natural elements around the site have to be assessed. For example, even though it is generally auspicious to have a hill or high ground at the back of the building, if the owner of the building's Element is of Water and the hill is of Fire shape, the hill does not enhance the site. It must be noted that man-made elements can be classified under the Elements; the theory of the compatibility or destructibility of Elements also applies in assessing the surrounding landscape.

FEIXING METHOD OF ASSESSING AN EXISTING BUILDING

The most popular method is known as the *Feixing* or Flying Star Method. This method reveals the auspicious and inauspicious influences on a building during various periods and cycles of time. Using the variation of numbers from one to nine, and by equating the numbers with the Five Elements, the auspiciousness or inauspiciousness of a place is assessed according to the portents of the Age or Era *(fig 68)*. Magic Diagrams reveal the changes in *feng shui* cycles every twenty years. This means that during the era of seven *(qiyun)* the magic number seven is most auspicious. The numbers nine and one indicate *shengqi* while the numbers two and four suggest *guoqi* (*qi* of the past). To assess the *feng shui* of an existing building, the birth chart of the building has to be noted, the orientation studied and the Divination Plates drawn *(fig A)*. A building built in 1985 is considered to be in the *xiayuan* and the *yun* seven *(fig 69)*.

The front of the building refers to the Water Star, while the rear refers to the Mountain Star. If the building faces north, the Water Star Magic Diagram is the *yun* three of the Water and Mountain Stars Diagrams *(fig 70)*. The Mountain Magic Diagram is the *yun* two of the Water and Mountain Magic Diagram *(fig 71)* By combining the Divination Plate and the Water and Mountain Stars Diagrams *(figs A & B)*, the final Magic Diagram depicting the auspiciousness of the building can be drawn *(fig 72)*.

The numbers in the top left and right corners of the magic numbers of

1 = Water Element (1864-1883)
2 = Earth Element (1884-1903) *shangyuan*
3 = Wood Element (1904-1923)

4 = Wood Element (1924-1943)
5 = Earth Element (1944-1963) *zhongyuan*
6 = Gold Element (1964-1983)

7 = Gold Element (1984-2003)
8 = Earth Element (2004-2023) *xiayuan*
9 = Fire Element (2024-2043)

figure 68

5	7	9
6	2	4
1	3	8

figure 69

4	8	6
5	3	1
9	7	2

figure 70

1	6	8
9	2	4
5	7	3

figure 71

1 4 6	6 8 2	8 6 4
9 5 5	2 3 7	4 1 9
5 9 1	7 7 3	3 2 8

figure 72

YUN NUMBERS AND ELEMENTS

1 = Water   6 = Gold
2 = Earth   7 = Gold
3 = Wood   8 = Earth
4 = Wood   9 = Fire
5 = Earth

figure 73

CHART SHOWING THE *YUN* CYCLES SINCE 1404

1404-1423 = 5th	1724-1743 = 3rd
1424-1443 = 6th	1744-1763 = 4th
1444-1463 = 7th	1764-1783 = 5th
1464-1483 = 8th	1784-1803 = 6th
1484-1503 = 9th	1804-1823 = 7th
1504-1523 = 1st	1824-1843 = 8th
1524-1543 = 2nd	1844-1863 = 9th
1544-1563 = 3rd	1864-1883 = 1st
1564-1583 = 4th	1884-1903 = 2nd
1584-1603 = 5th	1904-1923 = 3rd
1604-1623 = 6th	1924-1943 = 4th
1624-1643 = 7th	1944-1963 = 5th
1644-1663 = 8th	1964-1983 = 6th
1664-1683 = 9th	1984-2003 = 7th
1684-1703 = 1st	2004-2023 = 8th
1704-1723 = 2nd	

figure 74

MAGIC NUMBERS OF BUILDINGS' YEAR OF BIRTH

4 = 1996	8 = 2001	3 = 2006
3 = 1997	7 = 2002	2 = 2007
2 = 1998	6 = 2003	1 = 2008
1 = 1999	5 = 2004	
9 = 2000	4 = 2005	

figure 75

each square are assessed in terms of the compatibility of their Elements. The top right numbers indicate the health and personal wellbeing of the occupants, while those on the top left indicate wealth and prosperity. For the age of seven, the number seven indicates immediate 'happening' and the number eight, the next twenty-year period. This means that numbers six, five, four, three, two and one are distant in the future. Each number is associated with an Element *(fig 73)*.

In analysing the auspiciousness of any part of the house, the diagrams of the productivity and destructibility of the Elements must be considered and referred to. For example, the top row of three squares of the Magic Square *(fig 72)* are auspicious for the following reasons: One (Water) + four (Wood) is auspicious because Water gives birth to Wood; Six (Gold) + eight (Earth) or eight (Earth) + six (Gold) are not inauspicious nor particularly auspicious. Generally, numbers one, six and eight are considered good although it depends on the other Elements with which they are matched. The numbers two and five are considered inauspicious while numbers three, four, seven and nine may be auspicious depending on how they are paired.

In analysing the compatibility of the Elements, the time frames in *feng shui* are also considered. It must be noted that the Water Star refers to the acquisition of wealth while the Mountain Star refers to the sustainment of the occupant's good health. For example, in the square six, the top left and right numbers are one and four respectively, while the numbers one and four are quite distant from the number seven – consequently, both good health and prosperity are quite difficult to obtain. However, the square three is auspicious as both the top left and right numbers are seven, the number of the present era.

The *yun* (lucky or unlucky spells) of each of the twenty-year cycles of a building must be worked out systematically *(fig 74)*. The Magic Squares for the Mountain and Water Stars can be compared with the Divination Plate Diagrams *(fig A)*. A more detailed analysis of a building's *yun* can be made by assessing the particular year and month during which the building was completed. The Magic Numbers for a building completed in 1995 are listed in *figure 76*. The Magic Numbers of the year of birth of the building are also listed *(fig 75)*.

For example, if the building was completed in March 1995, the Magic Square of 5 *(fig 77)* can be drawn and another set of Magic Square numbers with 3 at its centre may be incorporated as shown in diagram *(fig 77)*. This square is derived from the Water and Mountain Stars Diagrams. The inauspicious combinations are: 2 and 2; 5 and 5; 2 and 3; 2 and 5; 6 and

7; 3 and 7, and the auspicious combinations are: 6 and 8 or 6 and 4 or 6 and 6; 1 and 1 or 1 and 4 or 1 and 6 or 1 and 8; 8 and 8 or 8 and 6.

FENG SHUI IN TRADITIONAL CHINESE BUILDINGS

Before case studies on contemporary building design are presented, traditional building design and planning will be discussed briefly. From this introduction, the relationship between traditional design concept and the philosophy of *feng shui* will be revealed. My book *Feng Shui for Business* has demonstrated that many ancient Chinese cities have been sited and planned with reference to *feng shui* precepts. The change of placement of major or capital cities was due to the change of *feng shui* cycles. In my most recent book, *Feng Shui, Environments of Power, A Study of Chinese Architecture*, comprehensive material and records of classical Chinese architecture in and around Beijing are included with particular references to the *feng shui*.

The palaces of the *Qing* era were orientated south because this was the direction associated with imperial rulers. The imperial palaces of the *Qing* dynasty *(figs 78 & 79)* were placed along the central axis of the Forbidden City with the back of each palace protected by the coal hill. The North Sea was created to enhance the *feng shui* of the Forbidden City.

The Forbidden City and the three main palaces – the Baohe Dian *(fig 80)*, Taihe Dian and Zhonghe Dian – were built in 1421 during the *Wuyun* (fifth period). The *feng shui* of the main palaces can be assessed by looking at the *Feixing* Magic Diagram. The small numbers on the top left and right represent the auspiciousness or inauspiciousness of the Stars. The right (the Mountain Star) portrays personal happiness and good health, while the left (the Water Star) is indicative of prosperity. In this case, the palace at the rear was sited at square one with Mountain Stars five. The number five indicates an immediate result as it represents the current *yun* cycle and the number four is the cycle before the fifth cycle. The entrance and approach face south and are represented by the square nine, with the small numbers six and five. Here, the Water Star five was particularly auspicious. However, the central square five has the small number nine on the left, which is not ideal as number nine is associated with Fire. Interestingly, during the Qing dynasty the central palaces were repeatedly menaced by fire and then carefully restored *(fig 81)*.

Beijing provides a vivid example of a city planned according to the precepts of *feng shui*. In this city, during the Ming and Qing eras, many classical buildings and religious structures were built in accordance with the practice of *feng shui*. The Tiantan (the Temple of Heaven) was built complete with auspicious *feng shui* symbols. The open-air worship platforms

MAGIC NUMBERS FOR BUILDINGS COMPLETED IN 1995

3 = January	6 = July
2 = February	5 = August
1 = March	4 = September
9 = April	3 = October
8 = May	2 = November
7 = June	1 = December

figure 76

9 4	5 9	7 2
8 3	1 5	3 7
4 8	6 1	2 6

figure 77

2 1 4	6 9 9	4 3 2
3 2 3	1 9 5	8 7 7
7 6 8	5 4 1	9 8 6

figure 78

figure 79

figure 80

figure 81

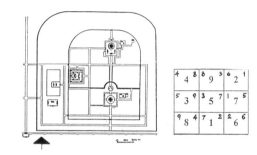

figure 82

figure 83

figure 84

for worship (the *Huangqiu*), was built on three concentric rings of terraces paved with marble. The plan and construction details demonstrate the application of significant *feng shui* symbolism. *Feng shui* numerology and *yang* numbers were used in the construction system. For example, the concentric rings of marble slabs have been arranged and used as floor finishing materials (from nine to eighty-one on the first ring of the circles).

When the *Feixing* Magic Diagram of the Tiantan was analysed *(fig 82)*, it was found that the main entrance was perhaps purposely placed so that it had the Water Star five, and its rear entrance had the Mountain Star five, as the date of construction was in the fifth cycle of the *Feixing* system.

Most of the Summer Palaces in the former imperial summer resort complex of Bishu Shanzhuang in Chengde were planned and designed with reference to *feng shui* rules. Built mainly during the Qing dynasty, the imperial palaces were sited on good *feng shui* land complete with *feng shui* landscaping. Hills, pavilions, crags, woods and ponds enhance individual buildings and the entire built environment. Eight lakes of varying sizes dotted with islands reinforce the *qi* of the place and space. Both buildings were built during the fifth *yun* with auspicious southerly entrances.

Twelve magnificent temple complexes are sited along the foothills east and north of the Bishu Shanzhuang hills *(fig 84)*, and thus are provided with fortuitous *feng shui* backing. Many other buildings, such as the Lihua Banyue *(fig 83)* are similarly sited.

The Danpo Jincheng (Emperor Qianlong's administration and main palace for holding grand ceremonies at the Bishu Shanzhuang) was rebuilt in 1754 during the fourth *yun* of *feng shui* cycle. From the *Feixing* Magic Diagram it can be seen that the entrance had the Water Star three and the Mountain Star five. However, the layout of the palace was based on balance and symmetry with a *Mingtang* courtyard *(fig 86)*.

The Yihe Yuan is another excellent example of the *feng shui* model of imperial palaces, designed and built with all natural and man-made features inserted for the enhancement of *feng shui*. The main complex (the Paiyun Ge and the Foxiang Ge) was constructed on the hill slope of the Wanshou Shan *(fig 85)* behind the Kunming Hu. When it was first built in the fifth *yun*, the *Feixing* Magic Diagram of Foxiang Ge revealed that it was placed at the site with both the Water and Mountain Stars five. The entrance building in the south had the Mountain Star six, but during the ninth *yun* in the year 1860, the Water Star changed to one (Water Element) and the Mountain Star nine (Fire Element). The Elements Fire and Water clashed, and during that year the building complex was razed by foreign troops. In 1891, during the second *yun*, the *Feixing* Magic Diagram changed and the Water and Mountain Stars at the entrance were two and one respectively. Ultimately, the complex was rebuilt.

The Leshou Tang *(fig 87)*, living quarters and palace of Qing dynasty Empress Dowager, Cixi, was built during the fourth *yun*. The *Feixing* Magic Diagram illustrates that the main entrance connected to the Changlang (Long Gallery) was auspicious. By 1860, the *feng shui* changed. It was obvious that the stars were inauspicious for that period, and that same year the palace was destroyed by the foreign forces.

The administration palace of the Yihe Yuan (Summer Palace) was the Renshou Tang *(fig 88)*. It was built in 1750 during the fourth *yun*, and the main entrance to the palace complex was from the east gate. This arrangement was not particularly auspicious and during the fourth *yun*, the Water and Mountain Stars at the east were nine and eight respectively. Both numbers were far from four and were thus inauspicious.

figure 85

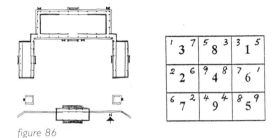

figure 86

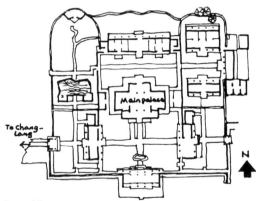

figure 87

figure 88

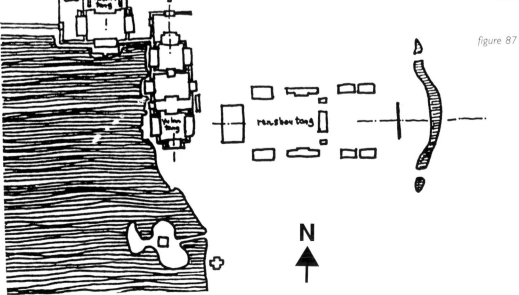

FENG SHUI IN WESTERN AND OTHER CLASSICAL BUILDINGS

It has been proven that traditional Chinese architecture is closely related to *feng shui* and the *yin/yang* theory. Some classical buildings in the West have been assessed with reference to *feng shui*. Very often they were found to be fortuitous with regard to the cycle during which they were built. However, any change to the *yun* cycle (lucky and unlucky periods) affected the *feng shui*. Many classical Renaissance buildings in Europe were designed and built with good *feng shui* orientations. Some examples are given here.

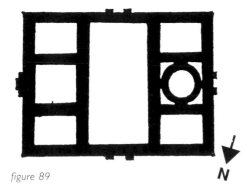

figure 89

Figure 89 – The plan of the Whitehall Palace, London (1621) can be studied and a Feixing Magic Diagram drawn with reference to the era of construction, location and orientation. It can be seen that the grand entrance to this Renaissance building complex, designed by Inigo Jones, was well placed.

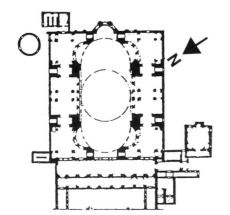

figure 90

Figure 90 – Hagia Sophia in Constantinople, built by Justinian as a Christian church in 537, was constructed during the sixth cycle. Its Feixing Magic Diagram showed that the entrance was well placed as it had the auspicious Water and Mountain Star six. However, in 1453, its Feixing Magic Diagram changed to the seventh cycle, as illustrated. Its entrance could not benefit from the lucky number seven and it consequently fell under the control of the Saracenic.

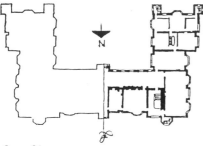

figure 91

Figure 91 – Hatfield House, Hertfordshire, England, was built in 1611 during the sixth yun. The E-shaped plan had two symmetrical wings. The entrance was suitably placed towards the auspicious south with Water Star six for prosperity and Mountain Star six for good health.

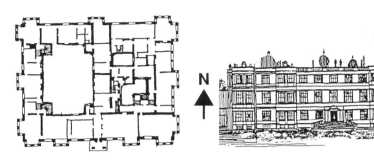

figure 92

Figure 92 – The main entrance of Longleat House, Wiltshire, England (built in 1580 during the fourth yun) was sited to ensure the occupants' good health. The plan has harmonious balance and is symmetrical in layout.

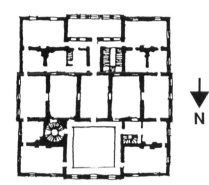

figure 93

Figure 93 – From the Feixing Magic Diagram, the Queen's House, Greenwich, London (built during the seventh yun) would best be entered from the north rather than the south.

figure 94

Figure 94 – Blenheim Palace, Oxfordshire, England, was designed by Sir John Vanbrugh in 1705 during the second yun. Its north entrance enjoyed the prosperity of Water Star two. Its plan was designed on an axial line with perfect balance.

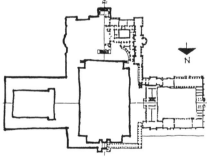

figure 95

Figure 95 – The Elmees St George's Hall at Liverpool was built during the eighth yun. From the Feixing Magic Diagram it can be seen that the south entrance was attributed with the Water Star eight for prosperity.

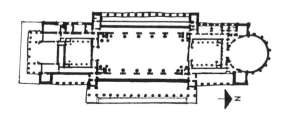

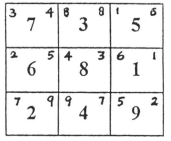

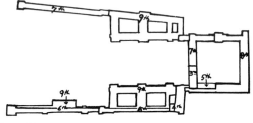

figure 96

In Paris many interesting and innovative buildings have been constructed, adding vigour and power to the cityscape. Of the many historical buildings and urban structures, the Arc de Triomphe, the Eiffel Tower, the Louvre, the Hôtel des Invalides, and Notre Dame Cathedral still bear the greatest symbolic and monumental significance and remain the main tourist attractions. However, the new commercial centre at La Défense and other innovative buildings such as the Pompidou Centre attract architects, scholars and others from all over the world.

The historical monument the Arc de Triomphe, built in 1806 by Chalgrin, is sited on Paris' central axis of straight roads stretching seven kilometres in length. This main circulation artery connects the Louvre, the Champs Elysées, Rue de Rivoli, La Défense and many other important buildings. These buildings and structures, influenced by *feng shui* and their *Feixing* Magic Diagrams, can be studied. The Eiffel Tower, constructed in 1889 for the Paris Exhibition, was designed by bridge builder Alexandre-Gustave Eiffel. Consisting of four bridge-like structural pylons it reaches over 300 metres high and can be seen from miles around *(fig **99**)*.

figure 97

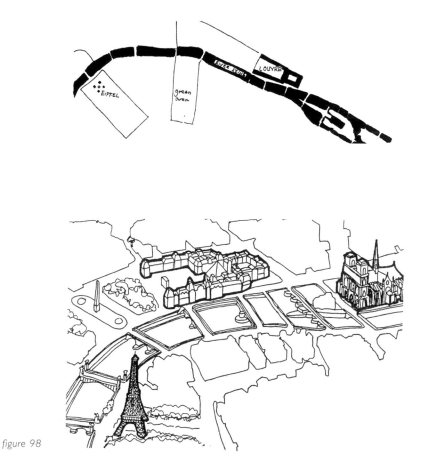

figure 98

The Louvre was first built as a fortress but was later converted into a royal palace in the sixteenth century and together with the Tuileries Gardens, constituted one of Europe's most imposing palaces. It was converted into a museum in 1973. The old facade consisted of two storeys with classical Corinthian and Composite pilasters, above which was an attic space. Over the last four hundred years the Louvre has undergone innumerable changes, exhibiting the progressive stages of French Renaissance architecture. *Figure 96* shows the various stages of development before the twentieth century and the *yun* of the various stages of construction.

The *yun* of the first quadrangle was the eighth. By studying the *Feixing* Magic Diagram, it was found that the entrance had the Water Star eight, which augured prosperity. In 1981, the Louvre was successfully converted to meet the most advanced museological requirements. Another positive *feng shui* feature of the Louvre is identified in its site and location along the banks of the Seine. The fortuitous relationship between the Louvre, the Eiffel Tower and Notre Dame Cathedral is clearly illustrated *(fig 98)*.

figure 99

The most impressive of the modern structures is the Grande Arche at La Défense, a hollowed monolithic U-shaped structure sited on a raised podium. The visitor is overwhelmed by the grandeur and monumentality of structure and space as he walks up the countless steps to approach the exhibition rooms on the base level. This modern structure recalls the grandeur and *feng shui* of the imperial palaces of the Qing dynasty (the monumental approach, the symmetrical layout and so on). Countless other multi-storeyed modern structures have been built on the sides of the axis of the Grande Arche. Magnificently landscaped areas, panels for the display of art work and decorative shops offer the visitors an extraordinary focus and sense of symmetrical space *(fig 100)*.

figure 100

As described in the previous chapter, the shape and form of a building spell its Element, with the combination of either auspicious or inauspicious forms. Generally, a square (Earth Element) is compatible with a round form (Gold); a triangle (Fire) with a square; a round form with an intuitive form (Water); a rectangle (Wood) with a triangle and a round form with an intuitive form. Similar geometrical forms are compatible with each other. For example, Leon Krier applied the geometry of two triangular blocks for the design of the Royal Mint Square Housing Project in London. In such cases the formation of both blocks are of Fire Element *(fig 102)*. Architect Oscar Niemeyer used rectangular wall divisions (Wood) to contrast with the triangular-shaped fins (Fire) for his building in Brazil *(fig 103)*. This is a harmonious combination of geometrical shapes. Le Corbusier used various shapes and forms for the design of his world-renowned chapel

figure 101

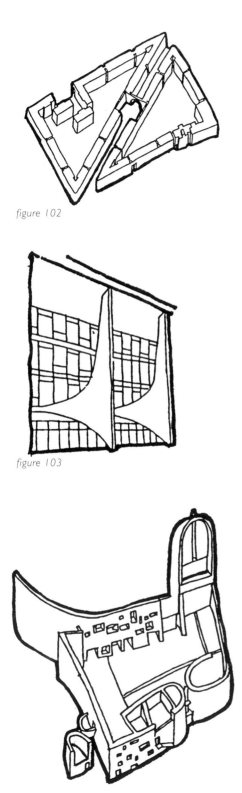

figure 102

figure 103

figure 104

Notre Dame du Haut, Ronchamp *(fig **104**)*. New York is a modern city with numerous high-rise structures and commercial buildings. The Chrysler Building, one of the highest in early New York, is crowned with Art Deco steel motifs of Gold and Fire Elements, neutralised by its squarish plan, creating an overall pattern of Gold, Earth and Fire, which is auspicious *(fig **97**)*. The shape, form, elevational treatment and proportional expression of the World Trade Centre, New York, is of Wood Element *(fig **101**)*.

FENG SHUI AND THE BURIAL GROUND

The deceased are associated with *yin*. When a living being leaves the *yang* world, seventy per cent of his soul travels to the celestial world while the remainder dwells in the tomb. How well the deceased are buried affects living descendants. The tomb, therefore, has to have auspicious *feng shui* to benefit the surviving relatives.

In ancient China, the wealthy employed geomancers in their homes for consultation whenever necessary. The burial of the rich and powerful was carried out with great pomp and ceremony. The choice of burial sites in terms of *feng shui* was assessed carefully by geomancers. It was believed that the *lingpo* (the spiritual energy) of the forefathers was linked to those of the descendants. If the forefathers were buried in auspicious *feng shui* sites, the surviving relatives would enjoy good health and prosperity. Numerous emperors, such as Qinshi Huangdi, ordered their mausoleums to be constructed soon after they ascended the throne. Qinshi Huangdi's tomb was designed to express the cosmic order of the heavens and the supreme power he held during his lifetime.

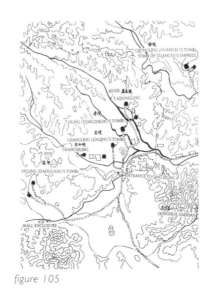

figure 105

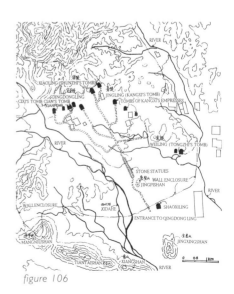

figure 106

The *feng shui* of a burial ground is enhanced by auspicious features such as hills and lakes. However, the relationship of the landscape features with the burial ground has to be assessed before the *feng shui* of the place can be summarised. Some of the essential features that influence the auspice of the burial ground include: *zhushan*, the rear hills at a distance; *shao zhushan*, the hills in front of the distant hills; *qinglong*, the high ground on the left of the burial place; *baihu*, the high ground on the right of the place; high ground around the place; the flow of water from the hills or elsewhere; the *qi* or energy of the place, and the actual burial place *(fig 107)*. The auspiciousness of the features is determined by the degree of harmony established between the different features, the profile of the hills, the balance achieved in terms of the Elements of the features and the quality of the *qi* of the site. Ideally, the azure dragon (*qinglong*) and the white tiger (*baihu*) form a pair of hills which meet at the burial ground site in the form of a horse shoe. The Elements of the hills are spelt out by their profiles and shapes: Gold is rounded; Wood, elongated; Water, irregular; Fire, pointed or triangular and Earth is squarish. The directions or orientations of the hills should be associated with the following compatible Elements: west/Gold; east/Wood; north/Water; south/Fire and centre/Earth.

The sites of the Ming Tombs at the outskirts of Beijing grouped on Tianshoushan, were chosen because they were surrounded by mountains and their south side faced low land. Such criteria fulfilled the *feng shui* requirement of having the black tortoise (highland) at the rear, the azure dragon on the left, the white tiger to the right and the red bird in front. The Qing Emperors adopted the Ming culture and practice of *feng shui*, selecting their burial sites with the help of geomancers. *Figure 105* shows a sketch of the aerial view of the eastern tombs. The tombs and burial grounds in the west were also built like those of the Ming rulers *(fig 106)*.

The ancient saying *jidi buke wushui* (auspicious ground cannot be one without water) stresses the importance of water features. Another saying, *shanshui xiangjiao, yin yang yong yi* (the hills and the water unit and the *yin* and *yang* are in harmony), reinforces the importance of the union and harmony of the hills and water to augur auspicious *feng shui*. The best *feng shui* burial ground has to be *tuhou shuisheng, beifeng beishui* (let the crest of the earth be thick and free from rain and flood). The Qing imperial burial ground at Jiulong Gu offers a good example *(fig 108)*.

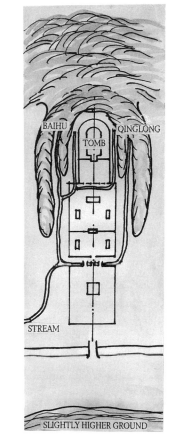

figure 107

figure 108

51

PART FOUR

HOW TO INTEGRATE ARCHITECTURE WITH *FENG SHUI*

GENERAL CONSIDERATIONS

The assessment of *feng shui* has revealed a wide range of variables: *Minggua*, *yun* of era, physical and environmental features, planning and structural form are but a few. In a world of increasing complexity and advanced technology, the assessment of *feng shui* must not be confined to *Xuanxue* (theory related to *Yijing, yin/yang* and so on). Architectural and structural considerations are equally important. The social and cultural needs of the users must be addressed; the functional and environmental aspects of a building cannot be ignored in the design of the tangible and intangible.

Although geomancers are not architects or interior designers, it is important that they have a basic knowledge of building construction and a good sense of design. If not, they may detect poor *feng shui* features or poor planning and circulation with reference to *feng shui*, but will be unable to rectify errors in terms of architectural aesthetics.

A building's external and internal spaces are subject to symbolic representation. For thousands of years symbols have been used in Chinese society – in literature, customs and *feng shui* – to express people's wishes. Wholesome shapes are good symbols, whilst unwholesome shapes represent misfortune. Squares (representing the earth), rectangles, circles (representing the heavens) and balanced shapes are auspicious, while triangles (such as an unstable three-legged chair), L-shape and other unbalanced shapes are inauspicious. If a building or a building complex is irregular in shape, the imbalance can be offset by adding an element. For example, if a house is L-shaped, either a tree, a light or a well-designed sculpture can be used to enhance the sense of balance.

Climatic and geographical conditions, natural light and air movement, sound and thermal levels affect the *feng shui* of a building. As different parts of the world have different physical environmental conditions, the following discussions will be general in nature. Climatic conditions dictate temperature, humidity, radiation, speed of wind and rainfall (water); consequently, geographical positioning is closely related to these conditions. Thus, in

Northern China houses and buildings are built facing the south so that the north-facing rooms are protected from the north wind. Those homes facing north are said to suffer from the ill-effects of poor *feng shui*. In the tropics where the climate is hot, wet and humid, buildings should be designed to protect inhabitants from the hot sun, heavy rain and dampness from the ground. Buildings with little protection from the elements are poor *feng shui* structures and tenants may suffer from the excessively *yang* (hot) environment or from rheumatism. In hot, humid zones, buildings should be oriented north/south with the main door in harmony with the owner's horoscope. In temperate countries the sun is a welcome asset as it brings *yang* to the *yin*. In such countries, large areas of glass should be used on the south wall to admit warm sunlight. An efficient heating and ventilation system should be provided for good *feng shui*. If these are interrupted frequently, the health of the occupants will suffer.

DOORS AND ENTRANCES

The doors and entrances of a building, particularly the main door, are very important features and should be suitably designed and placed with due consideration to their ceremonial importance. The main door, the most important element, must be sited with reference to the surrounding exterior and interior environment, the birth date of the owner, the birth date of the building and the overall plan of the building. The design and dimension of the door must also be geomantically auspicious.

The front door of an office or company should be designed to carry the spirit of the corporate image, be made of high quality materials and be located in a prominent position. The door locations in any building affect the circulation pattern. The front should not be in alignment with the back door; if it is, a screen or a wall should be placed to break the overly-vibrant flow of *qi* which may cause ill health or bad luck. If several doors are built in alignment, a chime should be hung to disperse the congested *qi*.

figure 109

KITCHEN AND COOKERS

Kitchens of houses and restaurants must be designed in a practical working triangle. One of the most important features requiring careful placement is the cooker. We are, after all, what we eat! It is important to place the cooker in an area of *shengqi*. This area should have a plentiful supply of fresh air to prevent any buildup of noxious gases and should be free of obstruction to allow easy movement. Most geomancers prefer to place the cooker with reference to the year of birth of the user of the appliance.

STRUCTURAL AND INTERIOR DESIGN

A good *feng shui* building must be designed with a sound structural system complete with solid foundations. The superstructure and the soil of the earth must bond and act together in perfect harmony. Thus, the structure must be designed with reference to the soil, the water level and the geographical features of the entire site. In general, poor *feng shui* sites for structures are areas where changes occur in the moisture content of the soil, where mining operations have weakened the ground or in areas of subsidence or seismic movement. Differential movement of the ground can result in structural distortion and collapse.

The structural components of a building must be designed to support the entire load of the building and resist stress. All load-bearing walls and floors must be stable, weatherproof, fire resistant and structurally sound. Most importantly, to avoid looking excessively heavy and oppressive, structural beams must not span too great a distance. Similarly, freestanding columns should be round to avoid affecting the interior with sharp corners which cause *shaqi*. Structural staircases should be designed to be inoffensive in shape, well detailed with suitably scaled risers or treads.

The roof structure is one of the most important elements of the structure as it not only affects the shape and form of the building but also the comfort of the interior. A complicated roof structure should not be allowed to exert a negative influence on the building. Where a roof is made up of heavy structural members, a false ceiling to the interior space can be inserted to counteract the negative *feng shui*. Dome, ribbed, folded-slab and other complicated structural roofs must be designed with discretion to achieve a harmonious interior and exterior environment.

High-rise buildings in particular affect the built environment as they can be seen from miles away. Several design and structural factors must be taken into consideration to avoid costly problems and the ill effects of *feng shui*. These considerations include the siting, structure, and elevation of the building (including the height and the cladding). For high-rise buildings, several structural systems may be used for load bearing and framing. Although the load-bearing system is usually economical, it is thick and heavy at lower floor levels. Lower floors command higher prices and are suitable for commercial enterprise but it is not necessarily advantageous in terms of *feng shui* as *qi* may be obstructed by thick, solid walls. In this respect, it is better to frame a tall building with reinforced concrete or steel frameworks to reduce dead weight and to facilitate the flow of *qi*.

The height of the building is an equally important consideration *(fig **109**)*, although it is often limited by economic factors, soil conditions, laws and regulations. Since *feng shui* is closely related to the financial considerations of a project, the most economical height should be decided upon after careful cost analysis, taking into account the price of land, cost of construction and the long-term prospect of return on the investment.

The symbolism of a structure is an important *feng shui* consideration. The structural framework should present an auspiciously-shaped symbol. Many buildings have been completely redesigned structurally because they were considered to be poor symbols by geomancers or *feng shui* experts. For example, the Hongkong and Shanghai Bank in Hong Kong was redesigned structurally because its structure, as initially proposed, presented a downward symbol. It was finally redesigned to give an upward symbol. Structural columns must be disciplined and must not be positioned in front of doorways, escalators, lifts, staircases and entrances. In open spaces, dance halls, large open offices, shopping malls, banking areas and other important commercial and business centres, freestanding columns should be round and structural beams should not be heavy, especially when they are exposed or positioned over important areas such as meeting rooms, entrance spaces, sleeping areas, banqueting halls and banking areas. In such cases, as discussed, a false or suspended ceiling can be installed.

Large halls covered by roofs supported by heavy structural members should be designed with care so that the structural members are covered to avoid the ill effects of *shaqi*. The loading and span of structural beams and columns must be economical, safe, properly detailed and aesthetically pleasing, all of which are good *feng shui* factors. For reinforced concrete structures, attention must be paid to the design and use of reinforcements and aggregates. Floors should be strong enough to bear all loading and must be fire- and soundproof. Staircases should be stable, fireproof and positioned so that they face entrances and doorways.

Structural roofs should provide full protection against the elements, be stable, thermal and fireproof and give shelter and comfort to the inhabitants within. In most cases, soundproofing is also a necessity. The choice of a roofing system is based primarily on appearance, costing, weather resistance and whether the system causes ill effects of *feng shui*. Heavy trussed roofs may be covered with a false ceiling to avoid the effects of *shaqi*. Internal gutters should be avoided on roofs because they may become blocked and cause leakage; the pitch of a tiled roof must be designed for the run-off of rainwater, and proper flashing must be provided at joints and abutments against parapet walls to prevent leakage.

An expert in *feng shui* should also be sensitive to interior design. In planning an interior with good *feng shui* he should remain fully conscious of what he sees within the confines of the interior space. The composition of form and space, the colour scheme, pattern and texture all affect *feng shui* in many ways.

To achieve a design which enhances *feng shui*, the geomancer must understand the principles of unity, balance, *yin* and *yang* rhythms, complementary colour schemes and compatible usage of materials. Careful and correct use of geometric shapes such as the square, circle and triangle must also be grasped to give appropriate significance to the space. Balanced spaces engender good *feng shui* as the practice is closely related to the significance of symbols. Irregular, unbalanced, awkward shapes are poor *feng shui* symbols. This is so because man, the user of the space, is a sensitive and conscious being who reacts consciously and subconsciously to the living environment. As he moves from space to space, he observes the spatial composition, proportion and scale of everything around him. He notices changing vistas, the significance of colours and textures, and auspicious/inauspicious shapes. The design of interior space is not limited to the shape of the space. The quality of the space is equally important as it affects the mood and wellbeing of the user.

The entrance space to both residential and commercial buildings is the most important and hence, should be designed and orientated with reference to *feng shui* requirements with respect to the owner and the surrounding environment. The imagery of the entrance space is most important, especially in a commercial environment. The colour scheme, lighting effects, signs and finishes of walls and floors all reflect the prestige and image of a company; the first impression is a lasting one. In the entrance hall, the reception area should be placed so that it is easily noticed and yet does not obstruct the flow of circulation. The desk itself should be checked in terms of orientation and dimension. The colour scheme of the hall should be harmonious, reflecting the corporate image. The waiting area should be quiet, comfortable and free from glare and heat. Displaying art works helps to improve the interior environment if there is no external view.

Functional spaces are just as important as the entrance spaces in a building. In a residential building the master bedroom is most important and should be located centrally, if possible, with due consideration given to horoscopic orientation or *Minggua*. The bed is the most important element in a bedroom and should be placed with reference to the horoscopes of the users. As one spends one third of one's life in bed, the blood circulation and *qi* must flow in harmony with the magnetism of the earth.

figure 110

Functional spaces in a commercial building must also be designed with reference to the users' horoscopes and the surrounding environment. The executive rooms usually reflect the importance of individual positions within the company. They should be placed in the strategic *shengqi* positions, in areas where communication with all relevant personnel is possible. Secretarial offices should be located preferably within eye contact or at least within easy reach of the responsible executives. Lighting must be efficient and glare-free. The conference or board room should be placed centrally and designed with a harmonious lighting and colour scheme to encourage healthy discussion and successful business negotiations. The dimensions of the conference table must be auspicious, and the chairperson should hold a commanding position, free from adverse influences such as the sharp corners of huge columns. If such adverse features do exist, they should be camouflaged with indoor plants, for example. If the room is not well ventilated, an efficient air conditioning system should be installed to maintain a clean, fresh environment. Rooms for high-tech equipment should be well ventilated, maintained and lit, free from dampness and fireproof. Open offices for clerical staff must be planned to encourage efficiency and order. The colour scheme should not be too strong (overly *yang*) or gaudy, while partitions should be erected to give privacy, a degree of noise control and a sense of flowing space. Work stations should not be placed below huge beams or oppressive structures. The important *feng shui* elements of office design include lighting, colour, floor finishes, furniture, windows and walls, ceilings, plants, art work and electrical equipment.

The location of a company's top executives, in accordance with the birth dates and surrounding environment, is important to improve the *feng shui* of their offices. Since an executive spends at least eight hours a day in his office, it is important that his sitting position is in harmony with the magnetism of the earth. The positioning of the desk and chair must take into account the orientation of the walls and windows, light and ventilation sources, the position of the entrance and the external view.

Lounge chairs and coffee tables should follow auspicious dimensions, and colour schemes should be conducive to a relaxing mood. However, chairs must be anthropometrically correct to avoid poor health or backache. The right-angled arrangement is preferable as it inspires conversation and the flow of *qi*.

LIGHTING AND DAYLIGHTING

Lighting is a major concern of interior design and *feng shui* interior. There should be just sufficient lighting so that the interior is neither too *yin* (too dark) nor too *yang* (too bright). Efficient and sufficient lighting of the right kind and intensity, coming from the right direction, must be provided for every activity and display feature. The *feng shui* expert should use lighting to brighten a defective dark interior with insufficient *shengqi*, or tone down too bright or too *yang* an interior to create a softer, more balanced aesthetic.

Too extreme a contrast of lighting should be avoided because it results in eyestrain and fatigue. Sources of glare from overhead spotlighting or reflective surfaces should also be avoided because they too cause severe eyestrain. Work tables lit with an even, low-brightness lighting system are suitable for office use. Glare must be eliminated from bright light sources, and from the strong contrast reflected off bright surfaces.

Although daylight is essential for personal wellbeing and for detailed work to be carried out, care must be taken to avoid glare from the sky. Such an intense glare can be reduced by the introduction of anti-glare materials, for example, tinted glass *(fig **110**)*.

FLOOR FINISHES AND EXTERNAL TREATMENT

Noise pollution and other disturbing sounds from the floor contribute to a poor *feng shui* interior. Consequently, interior floor finishes have to be chosen with caution. Noisy, hard flooring materials, such as masonry or tiles, are unsuitable for areas where intense concentration is needed or where the users and passers-by wear leather-soled shoes. For executive offices carpets are suitable because they absorb impact noise. For general offices, resilient floorings, such as vinyl and rubber-based materials, are similarly appropriate because they are noise absorbent, durable and easily maintained. A wooden floor finish is warm, organic and rich in texture and is suitable in bedrooms, for example, whereas ceramic flooring is excellent for living and terrace spaces where ease of maintenance and durability is required. The patterns of floor finishes are equally important, and in making a choice one should consider the suitability of the graphic symbolism.

The design of a fortuitous *feng shui* elevation requires well proportioned and detailed walls and windows. The proportioning and dividing of the wall surfaces of large and tall buildings should be subjected to *feng shui* dimensioning and should be worked out according to a modular system. Good detailing not only results in attractive, efficient buildings, but also ensures a better interior environment.

Windows provide the interior with views, light and ventilation, but if the external view is undesirable this could affect the wellbeing of the occupants. Window openings should be related to the positioning of the occupants for ventilation and good views, and window design should take into account the effect of weathering. Curtain walling should be designed with reference to the site's climatic conditions. If glass is used, allowances must be made for energy conservation and radiation. The glass panels must also be able to withstand wind load, their own weight and weathering.

Air conditioning units mounted on the external walls of a tall building should be carefully positioned so as not to create negative *feng shui* effects, such as noise pollution and unsightly elevational treatment. Poor *feng shui* features for high-rise buildings include the following: insufficient electrical power and inadequate provision of power points; inadequate ducting for services, resulting in unsightly surface wiring; poor heating and ventilation systems; glare on curtain walling or through reflective surfaces; poor planning of partitions resulting in the obstruction of *qi* and view; poor provision of fire/emergency escape routes; poor safety systems and anti-vandalism measures; building features that contribute to accidents; poor maintenance of services and replacement of worn-out service equipment; and most importantly, poor location of the main entrance door.

WINDOWS, WALLS AND CEILINGS

While walls define and enclose space, windows provide a sense of relief, a view, conduct *qi* and light, and influence the interior quality of space. If there are too many windows, there may be too much glare or *shaqi* and pollution. Equally, if there are too few windows, a gloomy, poorly ventilated, excessively *yin* interior may be created. Irregular, awkwardly shaped walls, poorly constructed walls or walls finished with inferior materials create interior spaces prone to the ill-effects of *feng shui*.

Executive seats should not be placed with their backs to windows because of possible glare for clients sitting opposite them. Windows are considered to be *yin* and solid walls *yang*; thus it is better to have solid walls as backing. A void at the back does not give a sense of security and it is illogical to build windows only to cover them with thick curtains.

Ceilings and ceiling finishes are just as important as windows and walls in an interior space. Over-decorated and low ceilings oppress *qi* and should be avoided in important spaces such as entrances, rest areas, work spaces and meeting rooms. Unless the space is palatial or particularly large-scale, over-decoration and ostentation should also be avoided.

In high-rise commercial buildings where mechanical and technological service systems supported by the underside of floor slabs or beams may be unsightly, it is logical to install a suspended ceiling to house or cover up the service system. Care must be taken to ensure that the ceiling is fixed at a reasonable and comfortable height so that it is not stiflingly low. The finishes of the ceiling should not be over-reflective or cause glare. Acoustic materials reduce noise and should be used for office interiors. In homes where reinforced concrete is used as a ceiling finish, the beams must not be too heavy to avoid appearing too oppressive. Light fittings must be well integrated into the design of the ceiling.

ELECTRICAL EQUIPMENT AND NOISE CONTROL

The placement of electronic and electrical appliances, such as computers, telephones and photographic equipment, must be considered carefully as they are sources of energy and noise; if they malfunction, they can also be sources of pollution. The wiring of these machines must be treated carefully, and heavy equipment must be supported by adequate structural members. All man-made equipment with the potential to cause ill-health is considered poor *feng shui*. Radiation from colour televisions, transmitters, X-ray machines and other telecommunication systems must be treated with caution as they pollute the environment and long-term exposure can create biological changes in human beings. Such potentially harmful technology should therefore be kept at a safe distance.

It is necessary to insulate buildings from airborne and impact noise by the use of suitable materials. Many countries stipulate noise criteria in urban and suburban areas. For residential urban areas the permitted level may be 55dB while suburban areas allow for 50dB. The *feng shui* of apartments must be ensured by providing insulated partition walls, resilient floor finishes and soft furnishings to reduce noise.

COLOUR SCHEMES

The colours of nature stir the moods and emotions of man. For centuries the spiritual aspiration of man was expressed by the use of stained glass in Gothic cathedrals and by the brightly painted columns and roof ornaments of Chinese temples.

In the modern context, colour schemes are proposed for interiors and exteriors to give a sense of identity and character and to create three-dimensional spatial effects within the building forms. The geomancer does not simply use colour to emphasise form and space, he uses it to create symbolism and a balanced interior. For good *feng shui*, a colour scheme should be harmonious – neither too overpowering (too *yang*) nor too monochromatic (too *yin*) – and compatible with the user's birth Element. For public buildings or those belonging to big businesses, corporate colours should also be taken into account. Warm colours such as red, orange, yellow are *yang* while cool colours such as blue and green are *yin*. Once the analysis has been made and the appropriate hue decided upon, two tints of colour at the opposite ends of the spectrum may be used to give a balanced scheme.

The Chinese believe colours have a certain meaning and symbolism. Red represents joy and good fortune; yellow, royalty and prominence; green, longevity and youthfulness; blue, spiritualism and heavenly blessing; black, sadness and sombreness, and white, a sign of mourning and purity. Traditionally, these colours have been applied on Chinese buildings to reflect the wishes of the people. For example, the Temple of Heaven was covered by a three-tiered blue tiled roof because it was for the worship of the heavens, and the emperors of the Ming and Qing dynasties called upon the heavenly gods to give their blessings for a good harvest.

On the one hand, sensual harmony and composition of form and colour add to a good *feng shui* interior, whilst on the other, colours can be used to disguise and mask badly formed walls and objects; clever use of colours can hide ugly details and badly proportioned walls.

SYMBOLIC ELEMENTS AND ARTWORK

The implication of symbolism and what people want their buildings to represent must not be taken lightly. Symbols and signs contribute to the identity of places and building envelopes. For example, government buildings, law courts, civic and parliamentary buildings should bear symbols representative of the institution and its achievements.

The best time to adjust a project for good *feng shui* is at the design stage; to change the sketch design while it is still on the drawing board costs nothing. It is widely acknowledged that even though the owner of a commercial or housing project may not realise the need for good *feng shui*, the tenants and buyers often expect the building to be designed with reference to *feng shui* theory; consequently, a building with poor *feng shui* features may not be fully leased or sold within the desired time frame.

Feng shui is the art of placement in harmony with nature. It is therefore important to introduce nature into an interior in the form of indoor plants. Plants bring *qi* and life to an interior, especially when it is entirely enclosed.

Indoor plants should be carefully selected so that they blend with the colour, texture and mood of the interior. The plants must be tended carefully and proper lighting provided.

It is often said that a picture says more than a million words; displays of art work certainly enhance the interior environment, especially if completely enclosed or partially open to the exterior. However, sculptural objects must be chosen thoughtfully and placed with great care in order, as ever, to optimise *feng shui*.

EPILOGUE

The practice of *feng shui* requires one to learn to live within the natural environment and to respect the forces in nature. The rudiments of *feng shui* spring from the timeless wisdom of natural science and geography. They can be used as a vehicle to achieve a better understanding of the natural environment, to develop a deeper respect for culture and to design a building more conducive to the habitation of man. They are applicable to different global cultures and it is timely that *feng shui* has finally become an universal practice.

figure 111 – The Reading Room at the British Library by S Smirke, basically of Gold Element

GLOSSARY

Azure Dragon one of the four symbols derived from *Taiji*. It represents the physical features on the left side of a site.

Baohe Dian the palace used for informal administrative work in the Forbidden City.

Black Tortoise one of the four symbols derived from *Taiji*. It represents the physical features at the back of a site.

Dui indicated by one broken and two solid lines, it denotes west and signifies the clouds and moisture.

Elements (Five) everything under the sky can be classified under the five elements: *jin* (Gold), *mu* (Wood), *shui* (Water), *huo* (Fire) and *tu* (Earth). The elements react with each other in either a destructive or productive manner.

Feng shui *feng* means wind and *shui*, water. *Feng shui* refers to the natural forces and it is an art of placement of structures on sites so that they are in harmony with the surrounding natural and man-made elements.

Ganzi the Chinese calendar is based on the *Ganzi* (Stems and Branches) system in which the *Gan* (the Ten Heavenly Stems) are combined with the *Zi* (the Twelve Earthly Branches) to form the cyclical sixty lunar recurrent years. The *Ganzi* system is devised so that each year is associated with a horoscopic animal symbol. This symbol was started by the minister of the first emperor of China in 2697 BC.

Gen one of the Eight Trigrams, it is represented by a solid and two broken lines. It refers to mountains and the northeast.

Gugong *gu* means past or old and *gong*, palaces. *Gugong* means the palaces of the Forbidden City.

Hetu it appears that the legendary emperor of China, Fuxi, saw a mythical animal appearing on the Yellow River carrying fifty-five black and white dots on its back. The dots were recorded as a diagram which was named the *Hetu*.

Kan represented by a solid line sandwiched between two broken lines, it indicates danger and refers to the north.

Kun shown as three broken lines, it represents the earth, femininity and the southwest

Luoshu Tu the first emperor of the Xia dynasty (2140-1711 BC), Dayu, saw black (*yin*) and white (*yang*) dots on the back of a huge tortoise when he was building outlets to discharge flood waters of the Huanghe. When the *yin* and *yang* dots and the Trigrams were drawn to relate to the Eight Directions and the Five Elements, a diagram called the *Luoshu Tu* (the Drawings of the Book of Luo) was formed.

Li denoted by a broken line sandwiched by two solid lines, it indicates the south and is associated with the sun, lightning and fire.

Luopan a geomancer's compass which contains many rings of information with a magnetic needle at its centre. It is set into a square base of lacquered wood and gives readings of directions, orientations, types of water courses, positions of Trigrams etc.

Lupanchi a geomancer's ruler divided into eight divisions each depicts auspicious or inauspicious readings. The geomancer uses it to assess the measurements of doors and furniture.

Minggua *ming* means fate and *gua* means Trigram. The *feng shui* of a place can be assessed by using the *Minggua* method. People can be classified under eight types of Trigram, namely *Li*, *Kan*, *Zhen*, *Xun*, *Qian*, *Kun*, *Gen*, and *Dui*.

Qi energy of the earth. It can be positive and rejuvenating.

Qian represented by three solid lines, it signifies the heavens, masculinity and the direction northwest.

Red Bird one of the four symbols derived from *Taiji*. It represents the physical features in front of a site.

Taihe Dian the main and administrative palace in the Forbidden City. It was built by the Ming emperor in 1421 and rebuilt by the Qing emperor.

Taiji *tai* means infinity and *ji*, extremity. Ancient philosophers created this term to represent the origins of things. *Taiji* gave birth to *yin* and *yang* elements and from it the Eight Trigrams were derived.

Ten Heavenly Stems each of the sixty-year cycles in the Chinese calendar consists of a Heavenly Stem and an Earthly Branch. For example, the year *Jiazi* is made up of a unit of the Heavenly Stem named *Jia* and a unit of the Earthly Branch called *Zi*. The Ten Heavenly Stems are: *Jia*, *Yi*, *Bing*, *Ding*, *Wu*, *Ji*, *Geng*, *Xin*, *Ren* and *Kui*.

Trigrams (Eight) ancient philosophers used the Eight Trigrams to represent the eight phenomena: the sun, the earth, thunder, the wind, the water course, fire, the hill and the valley. The Trigrams are: *Qian*, *Kun*, *Zhen*, *Kan*, *Gen*, *Xun*, *Li* and *Dui*.

Twelve Earthly Branches the Twelve Earthly Branches are: *Zi*, *Chou*, *Yin*, *Mao*, *Chen*, *Si*, *Wu*, *Wei*, *Shen*, *You*, *Shu* and *Hai*.

White Tiger one of the four symbols derived from *Taiji*. It represents the physical features on the right side of a site.

Xun shown as two solid and one broken line, it indicates the southeast and the wind.

Yin / Yang the negative and positive principles in nature. *Yin* refers to feminine qualities: the moon, the night, the valley etc, whilst *yang* refers to masculine qualities: the sun, the day, the hill etc. When there is harmony of *yin* and *yang* there is balance and wellbeing.

Yun Cycles it is believed that a man experiences lucky and unlucky spells during his lifetime. These periods are called *yun cycles*.

Zhen represented by two broken lines and a solid line, it indicates change and the east.

Zhonghe Dian the palace between the Taihe Dian and the Baohe Dian in the Forbidden City built by the Ming emperor and rebuilt by the Qing emperor.

BIBLIOGRAPHY

(Chinese)

Ban Gu, *Han Shu* (China), East Han dynasty.

Ceng Zinan, *Sanyuan Dili Tuwen Jiangie* (Taipei), 1965.

Chen Lifu, *Kongzi Xueshu* (Taiwan), 1960.

Chen Meng Le and Qing Jiangting, *Gujin Tushu Zhicheng* (China), Qing dynasty.

Ji Cheng, *Yuan Ye* (China), Ming dynasty.

Fang Xuanning, *Jin Shu* (China), Tang dynasty.

Fengshui Guaitan (Hong Kong), 1963.

Ge Hong, *Xijing Zaji* (China), Jin dynasty.

Gongcheng Zuofa (China), 1732.

Li Jie, *Yingzao Fashi*, vol 4 (China), 1097.

Li Jianren, *Luoyang Gujin Tan*, Shixue Yanjiu She (China), 1936.

Liang Shicheng, *Qing Gugong Wen*, *Yuange Shice Tushu*, Zhongguo Yingzuo Xueshe Huikan (China), 1980

Liu Dunzheng, *Zhongguo Gudai Jianzhu Shi*, Zhongguo Jianzhu Gongye Chuban She (China), 1984.

Liu Qijun, *Zhongguo Gujian Zhu*, Yishu Jia Chuban She (Taibei), 1987.

Liu Ruoyu, *Ming Gongshi* (China), Ming dynasty.

Lu Dalin, *Kaogu Tu* (China), 1092.

Meng Yuanlao, *Dongjing Menghua Lu* (China), Song dynasty.

Nan Haiguan, *Kanyu Xueyuan Li*, Chiwen Shuju (Taipei), 1976.

Pan Guxi, *Zhongguo Jianzhu*, Zhongguo Jianzhu Gongye Chuban She (Beijing), 1982.

Pan Guxi, *Woguo Gudai Yuanlin Fazhan Gaiguan*, Shanghai keji Chuban She (Shanghai), 1980.

Qinghua Daxue Jianzhu Xipian, *Zhongguo Gudai Jianzhu*, Qinghua Daxue Chuban She (Beijing), 1985.

Qinghua Daxue Jianzhu Xi, *Jianzhu Shi Lunwen Ji*, Qinghua Daxue Chuban She (Beijing), 1983.

Ren Jiyu (ed), *Zhongguo Wen Hua Shi Zhi Cong Shu*, *Zhongguo Gu Dai Jian Zhu*, Zhong Gong Zhong Yang Dang Xiao Chu Ban She (China) 1991.

Ruan Yuandeng, *Guangdong Tongzhi* (Taiwan), Qing dynasty.

Ru Jinhua, *Cining Huayuan*, Gugong Powu Yuankan (Beijing), 1981.

Shima Qian, *Shiji* (China), Han dynasty.

Tiangong Kaiwu (China),1637.

Tianjin Daxue Jianzhu Gongcheng Xi, *Qingdai Neiting Gongyuan*, Tianjin Daxue Chuban She (Tianjin), 1986.

Tianjin Daxue Jianzhu Xi, *Chengde Gujian Zhu*, Chengde Wenwu Ju, Zhongguo Jianzhu Gongcheng Chuban She (China), 1982.

(English)

Arlington LC, and Lewisohn W, *In Search of Old Peking*, The French Bookstore, 1935.

Ball and Dyer, *Things Chinese*, Scribrier's Sons (New York), 1904.

Bagenal P, and Meades J, *Great Buildings*, Salamander Books (London),1980.

Birch C, *Anthology of Chinese Literature*, Grove Press (London), 1965.

Bring M, and Wayembergh J, *Japanese Gardens: Design and Meaning*, McGraw-Hill (New York), 1981.

Burkhardt VR, *Chinese Creeds and Customs*, South China Morning Post Ltd (Hong Kong), 1982.

Chang KC, *Art, Myth and Ritual, The Path to Political Authority in Ancient China*, Harvard University Press (London), 1983.

Dawson R (ed), *The Legacy of China*, Oxford University Press (London), 1964.

De Bary WD, *Buddhism & the Chinese Tradition*, East Asian Institute, School of International Affairs Columbia University (New York), 1965.

De Bary, Chan and Watson, *Sources of Chinese Tradition*, Columbia University Press (New York), 1960.

Chao, Kang Chang and Blaser Werner, *China, Tao in Architecture*, Birkhauser Verlag (Basel), 1992.

Dore and Henry, *Research into Chinese Superstitions,`* Tusewei Printing Press (Shanghai), 1928.

Eitel EJ, *Feng Shui or the Rudiments of Natural Science in China*, Lane Crawford (Hong Kong), 1973.

Fletcher B, *A History of Architecture on the Comparative Method*, B Batsford (London), 1958.

Fung Yulan, *A Short History of Chinese Philosophy*, Princeton University Press (Princeton), 1963.

Geraint J, and Heard H (eds), *Handbook of Sports and Recreational Building Design*, The Architectural Press (London), 1981.

Hong Xunyang, *The Classical Gardens of China*, Van Nostrand Reinhold (New York), 1982.

Johnston RF, *Buddhist China*, J Murray (London), 1913; *Twilight in the Forbidden City*, Gollancz (London), 1934.

Keigthley DN (ed), *The Origins of Chinese Civilization*, University of California Press (London), 1983.

Keswick M, *The Chinese Garden, History, Art & Architecture*, Academy Editions (London), 1978.

Legge J, *Li Chi, The Book of Rites*, University Books (New York), 1967.

Loewe M, *Imperial China: The Historical Background to the Modern Age*, Allen & Unwin (London), 1966

Lindqvist C, *China, Empire of Living Symbols*, Addison-Wesley (New York), 1991.

Lip E, *Chinese Geomancy*, Times Books International (Singapore), 1979; 'Feng Shui, Chinese Colours and Symbolism', *Singapore Institute of Architects Journal* (Singapore), July, 1978; 'Geomancy and Building', *Development and Construction* (Singapore), 1977; *Chinese Temples and Deities*, Times Books International (Singapore), 1981; *Fun with Chinese Horoscopes*, Graham Brash (Singapore), 1981; *Chinese Temple Architecture in Singapore*, Singapore University Press (Singapore), 1983; *Chinese Beliefs and Superstitions*, Graham Brash (Singapore), 1985; *Chinese Proverbs And Sayings*, Graham Brash (Singapore), 1984; *Chinese Customs and Festivals*, Macmillan Education (London), 1983; *Feng Shui for the Home*, Times Books International (Singapore), 1986; *Feng Shui for Business*, Times Editions (Singapore), 1987; *Choosing Auspicious Chinese Names*, Times Books International (Singapore), 1988; *Notes On Things Chinese*, Graham Brash (Singapore), 1988; *Chinese Numbers*, Times Editions (Singapore), 1992; *Wind and Water*, Times Editions (Singapore), 1993; *Out of China, Culture and Traditions*, Addison-Wesley (Singapore), 1994; *The Design & Feng Shui of Logos, Trademarks and Signboards*, Simon and Schuster (Asia) Pte Ltd (Singapore), 1995; *Feng Shui, Environments of Power, A Study of Chinese Architecture*, Academy Editions (London), 1995; Lip E & Lim B, *Architectural Detailing in the Tropics*, Singapore University Press (Singapore), 1988.

Prip-Mzoller J, *Chinese Buddhist Monasteries*, GEC Gads (Copenhagen), 1989.

Needham J, *Science and Civilization in China*, Cambridge University Press (Cambridge), 1954.

Rawson J, *Ancient China: Art and Archaeology*, British Museum (London), 1980.

Sickman L, and Soper A, *The Art and Architecture of China*, Reinhold Publishing Corporation (London), 1968.

Siren O, *The Chinese on the Art of Painting*, Schocken Books (New York), 1963; *Gardens of China*, Ronald Press Co (New York), 1949.

Su GD, *Chinese Architecture – Past and Contemporary*, Sin Poh Amalgamated (Hong Kong), 1964.

Van Over R, *I Ching*, New American Library (Chicago), 1971.

Weber M, *The Religions of China*, Free Press (London), 1964.

Wilhelm R, *The I Ching or Book of Changes* (London), 1951.

Willets WY, *Foundations of Chinese Art: From Neolithic Pottery to Modern Architecture*, Thames and Hudson (London), 1965.